Wanderlust around the World

OrangeBooks Publication

1st Floor, Rajhans Arcade, Mall Road, Kohka, Bhilai, Chhattisgarh 490020

Website: **www.orangebooks.in**

First Edition, 2025

ISBN: 978-93-7426-989-3

Price: Rs. 440.00

Printed in India

WANDERLUST AROUND THE WORLD

CAPTAIN SURENDER MEHRA

OrangeBooks Publication
www.orangebooks.in

Foreword

Travel is more than moving from one place to another—it is the art of discovery, the thrill of adventure, and the joy of seeing the world from perspectives most will never experience. This book, that captures Wanderlust Around the World, is a celebration of that spirit. It invites readers into a journey across skies, continents, and cultures, revealing stories of flight, exploration, and the sheer wonder of our planet.

From the very first pages, readers are introduced to the complex and fascinating world of aviation. it is not just a matter of boarding a plane—it is a precise, coordinated ballet of aircraft and air traffic control to the thrill of flying on Indian shores. Flights from Europe to North America navigate carefully calculated tracks, taking into account winds, jet streams, and the need for safety across one of the busiest airspaces in the world. The book opens a rare window into this world, explaining how hundreds of flights move seamlessly day and night, each assigned altitudes and reporting points to ensure both efficiency and safety.

But the technicalities of flight are only the beginning. This book transforms the cockpit into a front-row seat for natural and cultural wonders. Readers experience the Northern Lights from above, the sunrise and moon set

in a single frame, and the thrill of navigating new skies and cities. The narrative moves fluidly from aviation to adventure, as readers are guided through iconic destinations in the United States, Canada, and beyond. From the bustling streets and skyscrapers of Manhattan to the cascading beauty of Niagara Falls, every detail is vividly captured, making the reader feel like a fellow traveller.

The journey continues to the magical world of Orlando's theme parks. Disney World and SeaWorld are not merely attractions—they are immersive experiences where imagination and reality blend. From Cinderella's Castle to underwater encounters with manta rays and sharks, the narrative captures the exhilaration, excitement, and joy of exploring these wonders. The book also highlights the educational aspects of travel, such as the unforgettable visits to NASA's Johnson Space Center, where the mysteries of space and the achievements of humankind are brought to life.

Beyond the grandeur of cities and landmarks, the book shares personal stories, cultural insights, and historical titbits. New Orleans' French Quarter, the festive energy of Mardi Gras, and the thrilling encounters at alligator farms all contribute to a sense of living the journey rather than just reading about it. The text also paints a vibrant picture of Texas, from Huston's energy and medical hubs to the cultural richness of San Antonio and Austin. Each chapter is infused with curiosity, respect for local culture, and the joy of discovery.

This Wanderlust Around the World is more than a travelogue—it is a celebration of human curiosity, resilience, and the thrill of exploration. It bridges the gap between aviation and adventure, technical precision and personal experience, offering readers a rich tapestry of sights, sounds, and stories. Whether a reader is an aviation enthusiast, a lover of travel, or someone who simply dreams of distant lands, this book provides inspiration, knowledge, and a window to the extraordinary.

As you turn these pages, prepare to embark on a journey that transcends borders, soars above oceans, and dives into the heart of cities and cultures. This is an invitation to see the world through the eyes of someone who has lived it, flown it, and documented it with care, curiosity, and passion. Welcome aboard—your adventure begins here.

Acknowledgements

As I compile the memories and experiences of my decades-long journey as a pilot and traveler, I am deeply grateful to all those who made this book possible. First and foremost, I extend my heartfelt thanks to my family—my wife, children, and grandchildren—whose constant encouragement, patience, and support inspired me to document these experiences. Their curiosity, enthusiasm, and occasional nudges rekindled my passion for writing and made me revisit cherished memories.

Special mention of my nephew, Rajnish Chopra, from Lucknow. He played a pivotal role in the making of this book. Rajnish, being the printer and publisher at *Lucknow Tribune*, took care of the beautiful cover design and printing with colored photographs, adding a visual charm that truly brought the stories to life.

I extend my sincere thanks to Prateek Tripathi, Cluster Head, Nuvama Wealth, whose support was invaluable in bringing this book to publication. Your assistance helped transform these memories into a finished work.

I owe immense gratitude to my colleagues at Air India and the Indian Air Force, whose professionalism, camaraderie, and shared adventures enriched my flying career. Their guidance and support allowed me to explore the skies with confidence and safety, and I am forever indebted to them for the memorable flights across continents.

Special thanks are due to the countless people I met during my travels, from airport staff and local guides to fellow travelers and friends abroad. Their hospitality, insights, and generosity made every city, landmark, and cultural encounter unforgettable.

I am also thankful to the publishers, Editors , who encouraged my articles over the years, allowing me to share glimpses of the world with readers. Notably, the Hindustan Times and Houston Chronicle played a role in nurturing my writing and documenting moments that I later included in this book.

Finally, I acknowledge the divine guidance that I have always felt throughout my journeys—whether navigating flights over the Atlantic, witnessing the Northern Lights, or marveling at wonders like Disney World, NASA, and Niagara Falls. This book is a humble attempt to share not only the places I visited but the joy, wonder, and learning that came from exploring the world.

To my readers, I extend my sincere gratitude. May this book inspire you to travel, observe, and cherish the beauty and diversity of the world.

THE WHITE HOUSE

WASHINGTON

January 24, 1997

Mr. S. M. Mehra
4023 Cypress Lake Drive
Spring, Texas 77388

Dear Mr. Mehra:

Thank you very much for your warm expression of support. I am honored to have the opportunity to serve our country again in this time of momentous change and promise.

I am proud of what we have accomplished during the past four years -- we have reduced the deficit, expanded and sustained economic growth, improved education and educational opportunities for our children, and empowered Americans to make the most of their own lives. However, we still have much work to do to meet our commitment to provide hope and opportunity for all our people as we approach the twenty-first century. As President, I will work hard during the next four years to uphold your trust, to protect our shared values, and to meet our common challenges.

Again, thanks so much for your encouragement.

Sincerely,

Bill Clinton

Preface

Flying has always been more than just a profession for me; it has been a lifelong adventure. Over four decades, I have had the privilege of piloting aircraft across continents, from the bustling skies of London to the scenic routes of North America, witnessing natural phenomena like the Northern Lights and experiencing the vibrant cultures of cities like New York, Houston, Orlando, and Toronto. Every flight carried with it not just passengers, but stories—of landscapes, people, history, and moments that remain etched in memory.

This book is a collection of those stories, a journey through my eyes, and a glimpse of the world as I experienced it from the cockpit and beyond. It is as much about aviation as it is about travel, culture, and discovery. From the intricacies of transatlantic flight operations to the awe-inspiring sights of Disney World, Niagara Falls, NASA's Johnson Space Center, and the lively streets of New Orleans, I have tried to capture the magic, excitement, and educational value of each experience.

Writing this book has been a labor of love. Many years after my active flying days, I revisited old diaries, photographs, and newspaper articles, piecing together memories that had shaped my career and my wanderlust. My hope is that readers will not only learn about the technical aspects of aviation but also feel the joy of exploration, the thrill of new experiences, and the wonder of our diverse world.

Whether you are an aviation enthusiast, a travel lover, or someone seeking inspiration to explore, this book is an invitation—to soar above the clouds, to wander across continents, and to see the world through the eyes of someone who has been fortunate enough to experience it firsthand.

Welcome aboard this journey.

Table of Content

CHAPTER – 1

NEPAL. FINALLY MANAGED TO GET MY MEMOIRS,WANDERLUST AROUND THE WORLD

Kathmandu, capital of Nepal where tourist attractions are plenty. A.I. (Air India) Jets regularly connect Kathmandu to India via Delhi. I had the pleasure to visit this town and surrounding town most prominent one is Shri Pashupati Nath temple in the heart of the city. Ancient temples and myths in the Valley of Gods, here Hinduism and Buddhism meet.

Kathmandu valley envelops three glorious cities–Kathmandu, Patan, and Bhaktapur. Earlier these were three independent states. Its exotic crafts have been seen in the Chinese culture like Dagodas. Its magnificent art and artistic temples, sculptures remind one about Nepal's golden era in architecture.

Temples of Swayambhunath is a must visit along with Pashupati Nath temple for the visiting Hindus. It is considered a valley of Gods. "Swayambhu" literally means self-existent one – Lord Shiv is the ruling deity and most of the temples depict that. As a visitor one must not miss the mesmerizing rituals at Bagmati, the holy river that flows through Pashupati Nath mandir. The arti or prayers on the banks of this river is considered very sacred. This arti in the evenings creates an environment of union of Gods and the devotees. Here also the cremation of the dead is taken place as considered to be very sacred.. This is in reverence to the holy river – Monday arti is considered very holy and right day to worship Lord Shiva. The foreign tourist can watch the evening Arti from across the river from the opposite bank. It is also a major attraction during Maha Shivratri and Hartalika Teej festivals. As per the Hindu religion and scriptures, it is believed the presence of God in every living soul which is called the Atma. It is an experience in spiritualism. Let us not forget about "Lumbini" in Nepal, the birthplace of Lord many times and enjoyed the most peaceful atmosphere close to nature with its snow clapped mountain range of Himalayas. Throughout the year, it is flocked by the foreign tourists and groups of mountaineers.

The city is 4600 ft. above sea level. It is primarily a Hindu kingdom, surrounded by temples and places of worship. The Budhha In LUMBINI GARDEN, is Lord Buddh`birth place. Buddha was born as Prince Sidhartha, In his early age, he had forsaken all luxuries of life and took Nirvana, Holy place for meditation. Nepal is situated at the feet of great Himalayas. I had visited Nepal many times specially after my retirement from Air India.

Mountain Flight to see Everest. LIFE TIME EXPERIENCE. MOUNT EVEREST SO CLOSE

Hanuman dhoka in Kathmandu.

well it is worth reading Now, I would like to take my readers on a Mountain flight in Nepal. Many flights are conducted by Buddha Air now, but in early 1996-2000 when I took these flights were conducted by Royal Nepal Airlines. Now, I learnt many airlines like Agni Air, Buddha Air, Simirk Airlines and Yeti Airlines have started these mountain flights.

These aircraft, depart early morning when visibility is good and no clouding. The aircraft after taking off heads towards the east climbing to 19,000 ft. It is a pressurized comfortable flight carrying approximately 30 passengers. Spectacular mountain scenery of the mighty Himalyan range starts. Many know of Peaks of Pearl but one waits for Gauri Shankar, full of spirituality depicting Lord Shiva and his consort Gauri at a height of 7,134 meters. Only in 1979, it was successfully climbed by the climbers. It is visible clearly as sharp and high on the horizon. As the aircraft moves towards further east, passengers get excited to see the mighty Mountain Everest.

There is Nepal on the west and the Everest (8,848 meters) known as 'Sagar-Matha' by Nepalese and one can see Lhotse and Naptse, Mountains besides, under it. This is the highest point on earth (Everest).

While flying east direction, passengers on the left side take a full view but passengers on the right-side sitting are invited for a view from the cockpit one by one. The plane flying at 19,000 ft remains about 60km away from these peaks due to strong cross winds when close to Everest. , one can see its majestic magical face so close that heart starts to beat faster. Passengers click pictures of this beautiful experience then after this view of 20 minutes the aircraft turns back towards west, home-bound on the same route. Now the passengers sitting on the right side take the full view. I was a privileged passenger, being Air India's pilot so was invited to enjoy the view from the cockpit on every three occasions. Clicked many pictures but still not satisfied and asked Nepal Airlines Securities to help and they provided a clear picture of Everest professionally clicked for me, which is attached for all readers to see.

During this flight, one can clearly monitor the route taken by the mountaineers. They fly from Kathmandu in a small aircraft to a small airstrip of 'Lukla.' Then start their walk up to 'Namche Bazaar.' Here in Namche Bazar they hire the sharpas plus all the equipment required for the climb Lukla to base camp, the distance is 38.5 miles. Trekking from the south side for Everest is more popular among the climbers as it is easier.

Trek to base camp takes about 8-9 days as the climbers take it easy to slowly acclimatize.

Adventurous tourists take Everest view trek. It is short and easy and takes 5 days for a full view of Everest high above. This begins from Lukla, they fly to Lukla and trek to Namche Bazaar and slowly to view point and back to Lukla and fly back to Kathmandu. Whole package is offered by many travel agencies.

FIRST HUMAN BEING ON TOP OF EVEREST. MEETING TENSING NORGEY FIRST INDIAN ALONG WITH EDMOND HILLARY FROM NEW ZEALAND TO CLIMB THE EVEREST ON MAY 29th 1953

Tensing Norgey Meeting In 1957 In His House Called White House In Darjeeling

I HAD GONE TO DARJEELING IN 1957, Decided to meet TENSING, visited his house and requested his staff, about my desire to meet this great person. Immediately, he was informed and he came out in lawn, where i was waiting. It was such a pleasure to shake hand with him and told him, I was a pilot in IAF and had come to meet him. He smiled humbly and though could not speak very clear English so tried in Hindi which he responded haltingly but he could converse. I asked him, how he felt standing on top of Everest he smiled and said Achha laga then i requested a picture with him, he gladly agreed. There was another Indian officer from the Indian Govt with him, so we took a picture which is ENCLOSED FOR READERS TO VIEW.

On my second visit to Darjeeling was in 2018, as a tourist, so decided to visit his house"WHITE HOUSE," I was shocked to see that house was locked, with shattered windows and in very poor shape. I was told that after TENSING`s death, his children moved out and settled in other countries and no one to look after the property." PICTURE ENCLOSED FOR READERS" that is life, when one is alive and famous, every one sticks to him but after, he is gone, even the near and dear ones find their own way such memorable events in my life gave me so much learning.

POKHRA - Regular tourist luxury buses drive between Kathmandu to Pokhra. It takes about 6-7 hours. On the way there are many stops, passengers can relax. Even regular Flights are operated from Kathmandu to Pokhra.

This is a lake city with spectacular scenery adventure activities and varieties of Hotels and restaurants. Great place to relax with a view of nearby snowy mountains like 'Annapurna Massif' and other beautiful peaks, specially the fish tail of Annapurna – I, II and III. One can hire a taxi to the view point of the mountain. From here one can see the beauty of Annapurna and other snow-clad peaks. In the centre in Pokhara is a beautiful lake and in the centre of the lake there is an hotel, tourist stay there the eccses to the hotel is by boat and evenings there, are very enjoyable with Naples Girls and Men perform local dances etc. This Lake reminded me of NAINI LAKE IN NAINITAL. There is so much for the tourism, MAIN ATTRACTIONS IN KATHMANDU in Nepal that it is just impossible to summarize it in a few pages. The main attractions in Kathmandu itself are Holy temple of Lord shiva, shri Pashupati nath temple, then Swoyambhu temple, Budha stupa and Kathmandu Durbar square. If time permits, tourist can visit Chitwan national park. Even few miles out of Kathmandu, one can visit Janak pur, Bhagtapur. According to the legend, Lord Rama`s Wife Sitaji was born and raised in Janak pur in Nepal but there has been confusion as per Valmiki Ramayana, the site where sitaji was born in a district in present day Bihar and brought up by King Janak, the king of Mithila and present day Sitamarhi is a district in Bihar but some say that Sitaji was from anakpurdham, a city in Nepal As a tourist, I would not comment on these theories but like the readers to enjoy other sights worth remembering.

On all my visits there from 1995 till 2005, I made trips to Various local places around Kathmandu to enjoy the Olden History and Beauty of this small country. Tourist come from far off, in the world and travel around. The beautiful city of BHAGTA PUR 'BHAKTAPUR, is only 8 miles from Kathmandu and is full of ancient best-preserved palace courtyard It was capital city of Malla Kingdom, The city features intricate wood carvings numerous temples and palaces beautiful architecture . I only stopped over a short time en-route to Nagarkot which is only 32kms east of Kathmandu. This is a little farming village but it commands one of most shinning views of the Himalyan snow clad mountains at sunrise. This is considered the best sunrise view in the world. I went there three times to capture this view in my camera. I stayed in a hotel called View Point at 7,000 ft. Early morning especially in the month of October, after the rains, when visibility is clear, no clouds, before the sunrise, one gets ready for shoot from the vantage points on the roof of this hotel, ready with their respective cameras. The Himalyan peaks from Nagarkot at sunrise are a magnificent sight to behold. This Nagarkot commands one of the broadest views of the Himalayas in the Kathmandu valley. This hotel, is on the hilltop surrounded by thickly forested hills of pine trees, an idyllic sight.

FROM NAGARKOT HEAVANLY SIGHT.

{SUNRAYS FALL FROM EAST TO THE WEST ON THE SNOW CLAPPED MOUNTAINS EARLY MORNING IN ORANGE COLOR, GIVES THE VIEWERS A STRANGE LOOK AS THE TOP OF THE PEAKS ARE ON FIRE}

The magic starts when the sun rays appear from the east side below the horizon and fall straight on the top of the mountain peaks in the opposite direction in orange glow as the sun still is below the horizon. This gives the view to the spectators as if the tip of the snow on the high mountains is on fire. Then gradually as the sun starts to rise the glow turns from orange to yellow. This phenomenon lasts for roughly about 5-7 minutes to capture in the camera lens. Nagarkot offers a green escape from the bustling capital Kathmandu and blissfully calm and laid back [picture taken from Nagarkot view point hotel roof top is enclosed]. This is a place to relax and enjoy the nature in the warm sunshine with a chilled glass of beer.

Hotels and food are cheap and enjoyable. I hope that this trip and description to my readers has helped to know Nepal and its beauty in nature better. Holidays to Nepal are quite affordable and the Indian visitors do not require any visa, etc. Just book a flight and enjoy the Indian rupee in exchange to Nepalese (at the moment 1.60NRE) Shopping in Kathmandu is plentiful in the 'Air-Conditioned' market in the center of the town with many restaurants serving Nepalese, Tibetan, Chinese and other cuisines. Here the 'momos' are very tasteful. People are very friendly, mild natured and helpful. Many people from Bihar are settled with good business.

CHILD GODDESS - This is a centuries old institution of the Child Goddess, a deity Kumari Devi, is deeply embedded in the culture of Kathmandu Valley, who's young, beautiful, decorous glimpse of Child Goddess is believed to bring good fortune. Generally, girl goddess is about 10 years old. She is revered and lives in isolated existence inside the house and rarely seen. It is the power of faith. I had the occasion to visit this house in 'Durbar Square.' They are usually from 'Newaries' family and they are Buddhists, she is considered Hindu Goddess. When they reach puberty, they return to the ranks of normal mortals. Kumari is considered the incarnation of Goddess 'Durga.' I believe that before the Nepal's monarchy was abolished in 2008, Kings would seek Kumaris blessings. DURBAR SQUARE '"HANUMAN DHOKA TEMPLE.

DAKSHIN KALI TEMPLE.

An experience to remember. There is 'Kali Goddess' temple, by the name of 'Dakshin Kali Temple.' Saturday is the main day for animal sacrifice. This temple is about 20kms away from the city in a village called 'Pharping.' I was stunned to watch live animals and chicken being cut and the pool of blood that was being offered to the deity. Well, I couldn't stand the sight of blood flow in the gutter and walked away. There is a 'bazaar' nearby, where people buy cocks for sacrifice. Not very popular with tourists but if interested in rituals one can experience this. Mosty popular with Nepalese people to carry out such rituals and carry the meat home as 'Prashad' from Goddess Kali. Well this is sufficient in my description of Nepal from a tourist point of view. Hope the readers of this book have some idea about planning a trip to Nepal. Let's fly on to another country.

CHAPTER – 2

IMPORTANT PLACE TO VISIT IN SIKKIM (INDIA)

NATHULA PASS IN SIKKIM[INDIA] OLD SILK ROUTE

Before, I forget as the memories keep coming over lapping, would like to go back to INDIA and mention, my ever lasting trip to INDO/CHINA BORDER and importance of it since it is the Gateway to mount KAILASH in TIBET under occupation of CHINA now. Among the HINDU MYTHOLOGICAL SCRIPTS, It is LORD SHIVA`s ABODE and considered to be very auspicious. In INDIA, people like to visit this MT.MANSAROVER. This PASS is called NATHULA PASS.

SIKKIM in North East OF INDIA INDO CHINA BORDER AT NATHULA PASS

I would like to fly my readers on this dream flight back to INDIA. This is a country of many religions, cultures, traditions, attires and food delicacies. One cannot be satisfied visiting north to south or even east to west. Let me start with one of my visits with my wife in 2012, to the Northeastern part of the country, Sikkim. We flew to Bagdogra and motored down to Gangtok the capital city, taking about 5 hours of driving.

Nathula Pass, this Indo-China border is about 4 hours of drive. It is located about 53 kms distance via most treacherous mountain roads at an altitude of 14,000 ft. If travelling between May, June, one can see cloudy weather, rain, muddy, broken roads, land-slides at every corner and water stream flowing from Mountain side on the road. Here one can see the snow-clad mountains of Eastern Himalayas. Temperature dipping to ice and high wind speeds are recorded. It is so difficult to withstand these weather conditions but our courageous army is manning this border post 24 hours a day. If one has to visit this place, then better to hire a four-wheel drive with an expert mountain road driver as this drive is different from driving in plains. Our vehicle was driven by a very young boy, my wife was little apprehensive about his skill in driving. But I must admit he drove excellently well with all knowledge of the treacherous road conditions.

En-route many times vehicles were stuck for 40 minutes to 1 hour till the Army personnel cleared the land-slides. Roads were not good those days but on my recent visit with my daughter, after the Army deployement, Roads are cemented and very good. But earlier, twelve years ago the roads were, muddy with slush and narrow, other side are deep down gorges, one shuddered to even look that side. Somehow, we managed to reach our first halt at Tsango Changu Lake at 14,000 ft. for a hot cup of tea and snacks. In fact, for Nathula Pass trip, permits are sold which are issued in Gangtok but can be arranged by the travel agencies. After halt of about 30 minutes or so we proceeded towards Nathula Pass, another 30 minutes for beautiful drive. Here at the bottom of about 90 steps and this takes your breath away at 14,200 ft. due to lack of oxygen. We both had to struggle and with some help from the fellow Indian tourists, who advised and also offered to share some garic flakes in the mouth to chew to get the breath back at the foot of the climbing steps, the entrance big gate has our country`s national flag and written on one side JAI BHARAT. we both could reach the top . We met the happy 'jawans' in their green uniforms and woolen caps and got ourselves photographed with them and chatting, made them feel at home with both of us. Here there was a chain between the Indian side and across Chinese side, the Chinese had made comfortable small room heated for their soldiers but our jawans were on duty in the open. Suddenly it started snowing in that bitter cold [OUR PICTURES AT THE SITE ENCLOSED] so we both decided to come down to our vehicle and drove back to Tsongo Lake, back to many restaurants for a quick refreshment and hot cups of tea.

Sometimes to remember of the tough weather conditions in which our brave Indian soldiers guard our borders.

This route was earlier called the Silk-Route for traders to China though it was opened by the Chinese and people from India were allowed to cross over to visit the great Mansarovar. Even vehicles were provided on hire from Chinese agencies to take the Indian pilgrims for a 'Parikrama' of the holy mountain considered to be Lord Shiva's abode. This permission was later on stopped after the Chinese aggression of 1962 but recently last year re-opened. But learnt, they closed this route again for Indian travelers.

Nathula Pass Visit Second Time, Recently 2023

My Grand daughter and daughter were keen to visit NATHULA, after learning about the History about it, so I took them to GANGTOK, after showing the city and its beauty and Buddhist shrines, hired a car for Nathula, when on my first visit with my wife but on my second visit roads were very good but during my first visit, while on the way near

Nathula, we had halted near a small Mandir it was made in the Memory of a brave Indian soldierHARBHAJAN SINGH, who had died in 1968 but still considered by the army people that his spirit continues to remain there to protect and guide the army troops from the Chinese troop movements, all army vehicles stop there pay their respects to Baba HARBHAJAN SINGH but this second visit that mandir was relocated about 10 kms at another site. Well, on my second visit i was surprised that near the entry gate another concrete diversionary rd was made to the top of INDO/CHINA PASS for only army/ military personnel. When i showed my military ID card to the Army jawan, he immediately contacted the office on the viewing gallery in charge and allowed our cab to travel on this diversionary rd. to the top instead of the normal route through 90 steps for other people to climb and reach the pass. There, I was met by an Army havaldar with due respects and taken inside the sitting room with heated comfortable seating, with sofas etc and hot cups of tea. Then he took us to glass enclosed gallery to view the border, of China and India.

Common people were down under this viewing gallery after climbing those 90 steps.

At that altitude of 14000 ft oxygen level is low and difficult to breath with climbing those steps for those people and in that cold weather specially. After our satisfaction, we were taken for a memory picture shot, which was framed in 20 mts and given to us. Then we were taken inside to the most important room where the meeting between Chinese military commanders and Indian Army commanders take place, we saw a big long table with chairs on both sides with Chinese flags on one side and Indian flags on other side. Really it was memorable sight which common people only read in papers. there were modern wash rooms on the back also.

IMPORTANCE OF MT.MANSAROVER REVEALED. LATEST FINDING BY NASA.

THE LATEST FINDING BY NASA, THAT MT KAILASH/MANSAROVER IS THE PIVOTAL POINT OR THE CENTER OF EARTH well this is located in TIBET, controlled by CHINESE. Indians, those who wish to visit MANSAROVER, take special permission to cross this NATHULA PASS in to china and, spl buses are available to take them around MANSAROVER for PARKARMA. every thing is charged in US $, I was told by some people. that no aircraft or helicopter can fly over Mt. KAILASH. IT IS WELL KNOWN AS PER HINDU SHASTRAS THAT LORD SHIVA`s ABODE is TOP OF Mt. KAILASH. Whenever there is some friction in INDO CHINESE relations, this NATHULA PASS is closed for this pilgrimage. ON our return, our cab driver took us on that diversionary rd Down towards BABA HARBHAJAN SINGH MANDIR {AN ARMY SOLDIER WHO DIED BUT AS PER SAYING, HIS SOUL STILL REMAINS THERE TO GUIDE THE ARMY ABOUT THE ENEMY ARMY`S MOVEMENTS TO PREWARN THEM The NEW LOCATED BABA HARBHAJAN SINGH MANDIR, it was very beautifully made by Army with HARBHAJAN SINGH IDOL and completely managed by army personnel, Car parking was made and visitors could go for Darshan and get Prasad of dry fruits from the army personnel. We returned to Gangtok and enjoyed the trip to NATHULA.

IN GANGTOK, MANY BUDHIST MONASTRIES ARE THERE, SPECIALLY. ENCHEY MONASTORY AND RAM

TEK MONASTRY well another beautiful place to visit is Bhushan Park where a very tall IDOL of LORD BHUDHA on a very high pedestal is made then another beautiful place is HANUMAN TOK. In GANGTOK another place to visit is view point from there nice view of the snow clapped mountain range is very picturesque, it self in the city beautiful gardens and big market is there, with nice hotels taxi stands etc. I Realy, admired the Sikkimese people, educated, well cultured, peaceful, helpful community. readers if visiting west Sikkim is also very beautiful spot for nature`s lovers. Cardamom is famous from there. Other places to visit from there are pelling, from west Sikkim Mt. Kunchanjunga is clearly visible well, on the whole SIKKIM is a beautiful part of India.

NORTH EAST-LADAKH

This will be interesting for my readers to learn about my beautiful flying experiences while serving under Indian Air Force (1956-1970) when I was deputed to Air India and subsequently absorbed in Air India and released from IAF in 1972. Just before I was posted to Agra Air Force Transport Squadron as a Squadron Leader. This Squadron was in the line of duty for mainly carrying men and equipment and rations to IAF. Forward landing grounds which became operational after the Chinese attack on India 1962.

I was commanding IAF packet C130 Aircraft DETACHMENT, from Pathankot to Leh, Thoise, Fuckche, etc. very close to Indo-China border. Except Kargil/Leh, other forward landing strips were very small and landing was very tricky with no room for error.

KARGIL, the approach for landing was around its famous Tiger Hill, one had to go around descending to land at a small strip at almost 9,000 above sea level. It was a military base and only IAF supply aircraft could land.

THOISE, it was another military forward base with a very small flat landing strip at 10,000 above sea level. I remember, carrying high altitude motorized armored vehicles and small tanks, ferry them to Thoise in most difficult of situations It is like a well where the air strip is made. Aircraft had to circle down descending to the airstrip off load the stuff and take off immediately again climbing circling up and get out and set course for the base at Pathankot before the cloud cover makes landing difficult at Thoise. It is real scary flying to those but due to the needs of the troops based there, it was most necessary as food and other military requirements were important... Sometimes, weather closing in with clouds left barely time to land, offload and get airborne.

FUCKCHE, this was a nerve wrecking landing field (airstrip) made on some perforated metal sheets and sandy ground, these perforated metal sheets spread out was to avoid the any dust rising on Landing to obscure the visibility for the pilots. It was at an altitude of above 13,500 above sea level. Only 2.5 kms from the Chinese border. While on approach to land, one could see the Chinese soldiers on the mountains overlooking the landing strip. It was very treacherous approach to land as there was no room to go around for another attempt and cloudy weather was a big hindrance. I always used to find at least 10 minutes to chat with our Indian Jawans in such blistering cold and minimum facilities. I had so much of sympathy that on return flight used to carry many of them coming back home on leave that sometimes take more Jawans than the permitted capacity. Could not see leaving them behind with tears in their eyes. But promised them for another flight next day if weather permits. Always brought their letters for their loved ones to be sent onward to their addresses. For them, life was worse than hell, missing their loved ones. These are the brave ones guarding our borders. Our whole country salutes their spirit to safeguard our borders in spite of bearing all difficulties and missing their beloved families at home Some time the letters, i used to bring back for their families, could lit up their hearts those days there were no mobile cameras, otherwise i would have brought their video messages to the beloved ones at home.

AMAR NATH CAVE FROM THE AIR AND NUBRA VALLEY VALLEY OF FLOWERS. HEAVANLY SIGHT

Once, flying from Fuckche to Pathankot, the weather started packing, clouds over the mountains. We used to fly above 15,000 with oxygen masks, etc. as these were non-pressurized aircrafts and mountains to Pathankot, had to cross over the mountains, with weather getting cloudy. NEVER EVER GET IN TO THE CLOUDS WITHOUT PROPER NAVIGATIONAL EQUIPMENT FITTED AND UNDER RADAR SYSTEM AS IT WILL BE TAKING A CHANCE IN CLOUDS, NO VISIBILITY AND MOUNTENEOUS AREA, SAFER TO KEEP OUT AND FLY ANOTHER CLEAR ROUTE. It was not possible so had decided to fly straight on through the valley on to Srinagar as the valley was clear of clouds. While crossing near Thoise, this place called Nubra Valley, I think only about 12 miles are little more from Srinagar. This is called the Valley of Gods. What beautiful flowers in all colors carpeted on the slopes of the mountains on my left. I wish I could capture that in my eyes forever.

Never seen such heavenly colors going for miles on the slopes. Now comes another big surprise, when my navigator told me that Amarnath Caves will be coming on our right in 5 minutes. These caves are at nearly 12,800 altitude and we were flying at 15,000 so I decided to come down to 13,500. Wow, weather was clear and clearly could see the caves and people in crowds. Summer time and beautiful sunshine, the heavenly picture was so clear and so close. We all bowed our heads in the cockpit and did Namaskar. Lord Siva had granted our wish. I hope my readers must have visualized the scene. We landed in Srinagar refueled and took off for Pathankot.

Maybe my sympathetic treatment to our Jawans, brought me the blessings from the mighty Shiva to give his Darshan.

LEH Since, I was commanding this Air Force supply from Pathankot to Army forward lines in this forward sector, had to attend many high-level meetings with the Army Commanders. So, had to land in Leh, Airstrip at about 10,000 above sea level and had to stay overnight as the return to Pathankot after the meetings lasting till afternoon, was not possible to fly back. In 1969, Leh was not opened to civilian tourists/airlines. It was only a military airbase, so had to stay in a comfortable army tent, provided with medical care, if needed with oxygen cylinders and masks. Well, one can imagine, what life our Army Jawans live in places like Fuckche and Thoise. From Thoise, they are sent to Siachin for further hazardous duties. This all, I wanted to induct in this chapter to bring to light that life is not full of roses. Only a few privileged ones enjoy these places now as tourists as lots of facilities have been made possible but in the late 1960s, it was impossible.

AIR FORCE DAYS, ALWAYS MOST MEMORABLE IN MY LIFE.

LIFE WAS TOUGH SOME TIMES BUT STILL ENJOYABLE AS CONTRIBUTING MY SERVICES FOR THE GREAT COUNTRY OF OURS. OUR SPIRITS WERE ALWAYS HIGH. MILITARY SERVICE TEACHES OF SO MANY THINGS, FIRSTLY DECSIPLIN, CHRACTER BUILDING AND RESPECT FOR OTHERS, SPECIALY LADIES. WELL, IN CIVIL LIFE AFTER JOINING AIR INDIA, IT TOOK ME QUITE SOME TIME TO ADJUST TO CIVIL LIFE. MY MEMORIES OF MANY MANY YEARS WHILE IN INDIAN AIR FORCE, HAD CHANCE TO FLY LATE PM PT, JAWAHAR LAL NEHRU FROM DEHLI TO BANGALORE AND BACK EVEN THEN VICE PRESIDENT LATE DR. ZAKIR HUSSAIN EVEN LATE PM LAL BAHADUR SHASTRI.

THE MOST VALUABLE PRECIOUS FLIGHT IN SUPERCONSTELLATION AIRCRAFT FLYING 'KING HUSSAIN OF JORDON" HE BEING A PILOT HIMSELF, INVITED HIM IN THE COCKPIT AND LET HIM HANDLE THE AIRCRAFT. HE WAS VERY PLEASED AND GAVE HIS AUTOGRAPH ON INDIAN 10. RS NOTE AS I DID NOT FIND ANYTHING ELSE[PICTURE ENCLOSED] WHEN IN AIR INDIA, AGAIN I WAS SELECTED AS VVIP PILOT AND DETAILED TO FLY KENYA`s PRESIDENT LATE DANIEL ARAP MOE FROM NAIROBI TO DELHI[PICTURE ENCLOSED}TODAY, I cherish LOOKING AT THE PICTURES OF SUCH VVIP`s AND DIGNITARIES, FLYING RAJIV GANDHI. RIGHT FROM JAWAHARLAL NEHRU, INDRA GANDHI RAJIV GANDHI ALL THREE PRIME MINISTERS OF INDIA. THESE PICTURES IN MY LIVING ROOM, Make me, FEEL HIGHLY BLESSED BY THE DIVINE POWER. RETD. AFTER 40 YRS OF FLYING WITH 16000 Hrs. "PICTURES WITH VVIPS" ALWAYS CHERISH IN MY MEMORY AT THIS OLD AGE" OF FLYING EXPERIENCE, IN AIRFORCE FIGHTING THREE WARS AGAINST PAKISTAN AND CHINA IN1962. GOD ALMIGHTY REWARDED ME AND PROTECTED ME IN ALL THESE YEARSAND EVEN LIBERATION OF GOA FROM THE PORTUGESE IN 1961.

MY MOST MEMORABLE SERVICE IN IAF WAS IN 1962 DURING CHINESE AGGRESSION.

I was based in PUNE, was newly trained on SUPER CONSTELLATION AIRCRAFT, which replaced our old world war 2- B24 LIBERATOR aircraft in 6 squadron. I was on a cross country flight from Pune to JORHAT and back. While returning, flying over GUHATI, suddenly ATC asked me to land in GUHATI, when i replied that I was on a cross country and proceeding to Pune, ATC replied these orders were from the AF commander positioned in GUHATI." {On landing as i came out of the aircraft, i was

accosted by a Sikh air commodore rank, don't remember his name, he came out of his tent. I saluted him, He looked at me and said" you youngster refused to. land, do you know War has started,"CHINESE have attacked. India," He ordered that now, I was under his command. He ordered me to fly to AGRA and start airlifting paratroops from there to TEZPUR and BAGDOGRA. For ten days, i was doing these flights from Agra, BAGDOGRA, TEZPUR, Jorhat. I remember, no aerial navigation and very difficult to fly after sunset as all mountains around some times, was so tired that without dinner slept in flying overhauls in the tent as early morning again had to fly brought hundreds of troops from Agra to forward areas landing bases as fighter aircraft could not be used. My wife, newly married was alone in pune, not knowing where i was for 10 days as it was very confidential she was crying and asking my squadron commanding offr. in Pune but was only told, your husband was safe, don't worry. Well, this service for the nation was, a very proud part of my life in IAF. After the Chinese halted the war, again, i had to fly to TEZPUR to bring back Indian POWs released by Chinese, they were completely brain washed by Chinese, during the flight back to DELHI, they were shouting slogans against India and Praising Chinese. It was very terrifying atmosphere during this flight, i had locked the cockpit and informed Delhi ATC about it. I was instructed, after landing proceed to military bay, where ambulances and buses were awaiting to take them to camps outside Delhi for De- brain washing. I have added this in my Memoiars so that readers may know the selfless service by the Army, Airforce and Navy in times of difficulties, these three wings rise to the occasion for the safety of our BHARAT. After few days US General chief of staff, Gen.

Maxwell Taylor came to India and wanted to fly to those areas in the north east, from where the Chinese troops attacked India. Again, I was deputed to fly him to those areas. He was very impressed with my flight, he had a team of few more with him with maps etc in the aircraft. He wrote a beautiful note in my diary about this flight.

CHAPTER – 3

AFRICA

Nairobi india flight to Nairobi via Eden adis Baba from Bombay in the late 70s Lingering memory, it is advisable that landing at ADISABABA is little tricky like in Tehran as the elevation of the runway is above 7000 ft above sea level and naturally the air is thin and the aircraft tends to float before touch down and eats up the landing length available. So, I had to be careful to control the flight approach and take the aircraft smoothly on the ground. After takeoff from Addis Ababa en route to Nairobi, always enjoyed the site of MOUNT KENYA enroute. It is the second most highest mountain after Mount Kilimanjaro in Africa with a height of 17,057 feet in Nairobi is modern and capital of Kenya. lot of Indian population is settled there, big malls, good five star hotels, foreign tourist flock here, for their African Safari, famous being MASAI MARA specially in the season. After rains, the migration of thousands of animals take place from high grounds to the plains across into Tanzania in Masai Mara. it's Safari lodge is set on the saddle of a Hill overlooking 695 mtrs of rolling plains, Woodlands, river. Annual migration is a site to see thousands of wild beast, zebra, ghazales, migrate to lands with green grass and Masai Mara village is to see that Nomad life. Travel agencies arrange even helicopter rides for tourists who can afford, to show them this show of thousands of animals herding down from high grounds.

NAGUIA LODGE [BEAUTIFUL EXPERIENCE]

This is in TSRO national Park in KENYA, This is on MOMBASA RD. About 140 KMS or more as from Nairobi it took me with my crew about 4 hrs drive. Staying in this LODGE is most memorable to watch the WILD BEASTS coming to the WATERHOLE under the balcony of the Lodge at night when all lights are put on and the visitors in the lodge have a beautiful view so closely. We had taken three cars on rental from Nairobi and my all the crew members accompanied me. We spent the night in the lodge for this life time experience. In fact, the lodge has a notice board at the reception, indicating the previous night arrival of the beasts at the waterhole so the guest get an idea, when to expect this beautiful view from the balcony at night. We were woken up by the staff at night as the beasts started arriving. As the flood lights were switched on, we saw RHINOS, LEOPARDS and other wild beasts. This was a fantastic sight to enjoy from the balcony. One can see BIG game without going afar it is worth a visit.

LAKE NAKURA

This is little afar from NAIROBI, few hrs drive to watch thousands of FLAMINGOES, giving the lake a PINK color. NAKURA National Park with shallow alkaline body of water, boasts of huge variety of animals including Leopards. NICE place for family Picnic.

KISIMU LAKE CITY

In KENYA, This city is like a Trade centre between Nairobi To MOMBASA because of its water and rail connections. There is nothing much for the Tourists here. Few safari parks. This is the Third largest city in Kenya because of its Trade centre.

NIGERIA

CAPITAL of NIGERIA is ABUJA, While flying for Air India to GHANA had a Stop in LAGOS as it used to be called.

NIGERIA is the most populous country but its political turmoils and instability it deterred any tourism. Main religion is ISLAM and **CHRISTANITY.**

UGANDA

Olden days, Air-India used to operate to KAMPALA, Capitol of UGANDA, I had fortunately, one flight to ENTEBBE, it was a beautiful place near VICTORIA LAKE, hills around, lot of greenery. Lot of Indian origin people were settled, many of them during big business, many Billionairs. After the military under IDI AMIN, took over, almost all Indian business men fled, most of them to UK and Africa, there was chaos, so Airindia stopped any flights. Now, I believe again under new Regime, things are turning normal but big business men settled in other countries. Africa has a history of rebels and military rule that's why only poverty and decline has spread. Uganda is a land locked country but diverse landscape and wild life also famous for Gorilla tracking. Kampala is on the bank of Victoria lake. Uganda is home to some population of Gorillas, I think some Hollywood movie also was made on it. Bwindi and its forest are the habitat of Gorillas.People there, I am told are very friendly It is one of the poorest country in Africa due to mismanagement. I heard still, some Indian origin people live there, who are traders and business in manufacturing.

NAIROBI:-

Air India flight to Nairobi via Aden, Adisbaba from Bombay in the late seventies has left a lingering memory. Adisababa landing was little tricky like in Tehran at high altitude airports and at landing the aircraft at adisababa, tends to float a little eating up the runway length. So I had to be careful to control the float and touch the aircraft smoothly on the ground. After takeoff from Adisbaba enroute to Nairobi, always enjoyed the sight of" MT KENYA." enroute, it is the second most highest mountain after "MT. KILIMANJARO." in Africa with a height of 17057 ft. Nairobi is very modern and capital of Kenya. Lot of Indian population is settled there. Big malls, good five star hotels, foreign tourists flock here for their African safaris.

Famous being 'Masaimara' specially in the season after rains, the migration of thousands of animals take place from high grounds to the plains across in to "TANZANIA." In Masai Mara, its safari lodge is set on the saddle of a hill, overlooking 695 square miles of rolling plains, woodlands, rivers. Annual migration is a sight to see thousands of wild beasts, zebras, gazells migrate to lands with green grass and Masai Mara village is to see the nomad life. MASAI MARA IS VERY FAMOUS SPECIALLY FOR FOREIGN TOURIST.

MT. KILIMANJARO:-

… is the tallest peak in Africa rising to about 19,340 ft. Thousands of climbers trek to the top every year. It is 200 miles, south of equator near Kenyan/Tanzania border. It is located in Tanzania, major tourist attraction. Tourists fly down then by road to Arusha or Moshi Tawns by vehicles. One needs a licensed mountain guide from a good tourist agency for the climb. I can never forget the beautiful Hollywood film made in 1952, "Snows of Kilimanjaro" with Gregory Park, Ava Gardener and Susan Hayward. {HOPE

SOME OF MY READERS HAVE SEEN THIS GREAT MOVIE, STILL THEY CAN WATCH ON YOU TUBE"}.

LAKE NAKURA:-

It is few hours drive from Nairobi to watch thousands of Flamingos, giving the lake a pink shimmering color. Lake Nakura National Park with shallow alkaline body of water, this boasts of huge variety of animals including Leopards. Nice place for a family picnic. My local friend had a arranged a picnic there with food etc.

KISIMU LAKE CITY ON VICTORYA LAKE---------

In KENYA, this city is like a trade centre between lake victoria and Mombasa because of its water and rail connections. There is nothing much as a tourist so, nothing else to mention. There are few places for tourists for wild safari park etc. Nothing much It is third Largest City in Kenya.

NIGERIA:-

Capital of Nigeria is Abuja, Air India flights to Accra in Ghana had a stopover in Lagos. Nigeria is the most populous African country but its political turmoils and instability deterred any tourism. Main religion is Islam and Christianity. I never stayed during my flights there but flew out to Accra in Ghana, where we had a long layover.

ACCRA:-

It is the capital of Ghana and quite populous but for us the Air India crew was not much to venture out. Here, there is Kwame Nkrumah Memorial Park, he was Ghana's founding father and a peace gospel. I remember, once I got stuck there with my crew for 7 days as there was a military takeover by flight Lt. Rawlings in 1979. My crew and I had befriended the local Indian community so it was easy to be invited by them and enjoyed

their hospitality. I had somehow the knack of getting stuck on three occasions during a military coup or civilian revolution. I remember getting stuck even in Tehran.

In 1979 also in Beirut when Arab Israel 5 days war had started. I cannot forget one of my Accra Flights. I was checking one of the new commanders on that route. We used to fly, from Nairobi to Lagos, now the name is changed to ABUJA [NIGERIA], after short halt, our flight to Accra, [GHANA] was about two hrs. On this particular flight, when almost 60 miles from destination, we were warned about the Desert Storm called Harmattan, approaching Accra and effecting Visibility, There was no instrument landing System those days at acc a Air port. I encouraged the capt. under check not to worr, just fly accurately on Visual Omni Range [VOR] landing SYSTEM, Now it was one chance, if failed, we had only one alternate to divert to Abidjan on the Ivory coast. Well i kept a watch on the latest visibility on the airfield from accra f light control, listening and Ready to make the final approach. Only about 2 miles from the runway found it slightly on our right but sighting runway was a relief, immediately made a sharp turn to align about 2 miles from the runway found it slightly on our right but sighting runway was a with runway as the desert winds had already covered other end of the runway. Some how managed to touch down before the whole runway was covered. That was really a touch and go situation. We were stuck there in accra for almost 5 days, when all cleared and our Airiindia flight from Nairobi Arrived and we took the return flight back. Such incidents leave a lasting memory for a Flight capt.

ACCRA. MILITARY COUP BY RAWLINGS. STUCK THERE FOR A WEEK, WITHOUT ANY SOURCE OF FOOD AS COMPLETE LOCK DOWN. THESE OLD MEMORIES CRAWL BACK. SUCH EXPERIENCES ARE IMBIBED IN THE BRAIN IMBIBED IN THE BRAIN.

ACCRA {GHANA}

It is the Capital of GHANA and quite populous but not much as crew of Air India to venture out. THERE IS KWAMA NKRUMA MEMORIAL PARK, he was Ghana`s founding father and a Peace Gospel. I remember, once I got stuck there with my It is the Capital of GHANA and quite populous but not much as crew of Air India to venture out. THERE IS KWAMA NKRUMA MEMORIAL PARK, he was Ghana`s founding father and a Peace Gospel. I remember, once I got stuck there with my crew for seven days as there was a military takeover by flight Lt. Rawlings in 1979. There was no food around as the complete shut down in the town. Fortunately, I had been friendly with the local Indian community, so it was easy to be invited by them and enjoyed their hospitality, Unfortunately, I have lack of getting stuck on three occasions during military revolutions. I remember getting stuck in Tehran in 1979 when the Shah of Iran fled the country and Khomeini had taken over, then in Beirut when Arab Israel war took place, five days war had started ANOTHER EXPERIENCE. I cannot forget one of my Air India flight. I was checking one of the Flight commanders, that route we used to fly from Nairobi to LEGOS. Now the name is to Abuja after short halt halt, flight to Ghana.

We were , on this particular flight when almost 60 miles from destination we were informed, about the Desert storm called Harmada, approaching airport, affecting visibility, there was no instrument landing system those days at airport, I told the Capt under check, As i was the check pilot sitting in co-pilot seat, not to worry, just fly accurately on visual Omni range VOR landing system, As the storm was approaching fast and the visibility on the airfield was reducing, we were hoping to land fast before the runway was covered up these desert winds were reducing the visibility and we had only one chance to try to land otherwise had to divert to IVORY COAST. While descending for the final approach, I saw Runway lights just 2 miles to the right, immediately took control and corrective action and lined up with runway approach lights to touch down in time before the visibility clamped down. It was a touch and go situation well, i mentioned this in this book for my readers to get little thrill as to how the Capt in the cockpit visualises for the safety of his passengers. well we were stuck there more than 5 days till weather cleared and Air India flight came and we took the return flt to Nairobi.

Such incidents leave a mark in the memory of a Retd pilot, when he looks back during his Flying days.

TANZANIA

MASAI MARA

Visiting Masai Mara is a treat when the animal migration of wild beasts take place which is between the month of May and June till October. When the rains are over and dry season starts in Sarangeti national park in Tanzania and millions of wild beasts move from North to south.

Towards Masai Mara on the border of Kenya and Tanzania in search of grasslands and water. Thousands of wild beasts, zebras and gazelles migrate. In fact, millions of animals move from south of Tanzania to the north towards Masai Mara. Visitors from Nairobi travel by Taxis/Domestic flights through tours which includes hotels, food and guide. Most of the visitors are foreigners from the West.

Another interesting tour for the visitors is the tour to Mt. Kilimanjaro again through travel agencies in Tazmania. What little bit of my experience in Africa, I must say it was worth remembering for life.

MADAGASCAR

IT IS AN AFRICAN ISLAND COUNTRYWHICH IS ABOUT 1000 MILES BY FLIGHT BUT IT DEPENDS WHICH AIRPORT IN MADAGASCAR AS THIS ISLAND SPREADS DOWN AND ALMOST NEAR MOPUTU.

IN MAGADISIO, THERE IT IS ABOUT 750 MILES. IT POPULATION IS MOSTLY PROTESTANT CHRISTIANS AND SOM MUSLIMS, IT HAS SERENE BEAUTIFUL BEACHES AND FAMOUS FOR ITS LEMURS, THAT ANIMAL IS ONLY FOUND THERE.PEOPLE ARE FRIENDLY. MAINLY TOURIST FROM EUROPIAN COUNTRIES DO VISIT BUT I HAD NO OPPORTUNITY DURING MY STAYAND NOT INTERESTED. ITS CLOVES CULTIVATION AND OTHER SPICES ARE FAMOUS.

AFTER RETIREMENT FROM AIR INDIA1994, ONCE WENT ON A HOLIDAY FOR 10 DAYS TO DAR ES SALAAM AS MY NIECE LIVED THERE AND BOTH HUSBAND AND WIFE INSISTED TO VISIT THEM. PROMISED FOR A TRIP TO SAFARI PARK I WAS VERY INTERESTED FOR THAT OFFER. I WAS LOOKING FORWARD TO ENJOY ONE OF THE AFRICAN SAFARIES THERE.

RUAHA NATIONAL SAFARI PARK.

IT WAS AN EXPERIENCE TO VISIT AN AFRICAN SAFARI, SO MY HOSTS DECIDED TO TAKE ME TO THIS PARK, WHICH WAS ABOUT 250 MILES BY ROAD. WELL WE ARRIVED THERE IN ABOUT 4 HRS AND STAYED IN A LODGE CLOSE TO THIS PARK, NEXT MORNING, AFTER B`FAST WE LEFT AND TOOK OUR OWN CAR AND HIRED A GUIDE FROM THE PARK. THIS PARK IS FAMOUS FOR LIONS, LEAPORDS AND LARGE GROUPS OF ELEPHANTS AND ANTELOPS PLUS OTHER HERDS OF WILD BUFFLOS. DIFFERENT SPECIES OF BIRDS, REAL FUN TO WATCH THEM CLOSESLY. I WILL NEVER FORGET THE INCIDENT THERE SINCE THE TRACKS IN THAT PARK WERE UNEVEN AND ONE HAD TO DRIVE CAREFULLY BUT AT ONE PLACE THE CAR JUMPED AND WENT THROUGH AN UNEVEN PLACE, SUDDENLY, WE FOUND ITS SILENCER HAD BROKEN FROM THE REAR SIDE. WE HAD TO STOP AND ASKED THE GUIDE TO GET OUT AND SEE WHAT COULD BE DONE. HE REFUSED TO GET OUT. HE WAS SO AFRAID OF THAT LOCATION WITH WILD BEASTS. THERE WAS NO ALTERNATIVE BUT MYSELF AND MY SON-IN-LAW, WHO WAS DRIVING GOT OUT AND FOUND THE SILENCER OF THE CAR HANGING. I SUGGESTED TO TAKE A WOODEN SMALL BRANCH FROM A TREES AND TIE IT WITH A CLOTH. AS THE SILENCER WAS HOT, WE TRIED AND TIED IT AND SLOWLY MOVED AHEAD. REALLY IT WAS SO SCARRY BUT NO OTHER CHOICE WE SAW SOME LIONS

QUIETLY SITTING, HERDS OF BUFFLOS AND VAST GROUPS OF ELEPHANTS AND ANTELOPS, ALMOST WHOLE DAY WE ENJOYED AND THEN GOT THE SILENCER REPAIRED AND RETURNED TO THE LODGE BEFORE SUNSET AND NEXT DAY BACK TO DAR ES SALAAM WHAT AN EXPERIENCE. COULD NOT GO TO SARRENGETTI SAFARi AS IT WAS TOO FAR.

ZIMBABWE (VICTORIA FALLS):- WHILE FLYING FOR AIR INDIA.

My Air India flight took me to Zimbabwe also. It was Harare, the capital city. Very neat and clean, old Salisbury. In fact, I remember it for its Zambezi river which makes Victoria Falls in a town called Livingstone. Regular flights go there from Harare. Earlier Zimbabwe was known as Southern Rodesia. It was old British colony. In 1980, it gained Independence from the British. It is a landlocked country with Zambia in the North, Botswana in the West, South Africa in the South and Mozambique in the East.

It is very interesting to know more about African countries, their cuture, their habits, etc. I had done many flights for many years from Air India as well with Air Mauritius. Today, many people do not know much about African Continent but it has many potentials for progress and development. Many western countries ruled over them and military dictatorships did not allow any prosperity. {We all know The regime of ADI AMIN in Uganda. All top Indian Businessmen and Industrialists fled the country by his terrible military regime}.

<u>VICTORIA FALLS</u>

Well, coming back to Zimbabwe, I would like to mention about my trip to Livingstone and Victoria Falls. ONE flight to HARARE, we had a lay over for 4 days. We used to stay in Hotel MONOMOTAPA they had their hotel in Living stone also near LAKE VICTORIA FALLS. I requested our Air India mgr if possible to get me complimentary tkts with my son on AIR ZIMBABWE, to LIVING STONE, an opportunity to visit Victoria falls.

Fortunately, he managed then i requested our hotel MONOMOTAPA, if i could check out in Harare and check in in their hotel in Living stone, they agreed and we flew to living stone by AIR ZIMBABVE and checked in hotel MONOMOTAPA same afternoon, hardly half a km from VICTORIA FALLS. What a thrilling experience, then at night enjoyed dinner in the hotel with African dancing show. Next day since Sunday, there were two flats by Air ZIMBABVE. so my crew could also avail complimentary tkts and joined me again we visited together Victoria falls and flew back to gather to HARARE. Well, worth remembering visiting VICTORIA FALLS. {MY CABIN CREW WAS MUCH DELIGHTED}.

FLIGHT TO ACCRA:-

Flight from Nairobi to Accra in the late 1970s, I had a very scary experience with sudden visibility reducing due to some weather phenomena. I was checking a commander on 707 boeing for his clearance on the route. Since, I was the right- hand co-pilot seat so had to only monitor, the commander under-checked. I was only 60 miles from Accra airport when Air Traffic Control informed that the visibility was dropping very fast. This was an alarm to prepare for an alternate airport for diversion. This weather phenomena are known as 'Harmattan.' The dust raising winds from Sahara deserts start collecting thick sand particles of dust and move from North East towards Westerly direction obstructing the sunlight completely. I gave confidence to the pilot undercheck that I shall help him to safely land before this weather completely engulfs Accra Airport. Those days the Southies did not have ILS landing system and only Visual Omni Range system were available which had its own limitations for visibility, so had to visually see the runway at least from 1200 to 1500 meters visibility (ILS needs only 300 meters but improved version can guide the aircraft landing to zero level on ground). So, I kept checking the VOR needle to be kept in the center in line with the runway and kept guiding the captain, undercheck to fly accurately, tilted 5 degrees to the left/right would take us on the coming runway 2/3 miles, so it had to be very accurate flying.

He had to look straight ahead and I had to watch VOR needle in the center and both my navigator and flight engineer were to look for runway lights. In the meantime, we had prepared for diversion after one over shoot to Abitfan on the very coast. As my luck would have it, we spotted the runway at Accra first little to our right at 1500 ft. One try, that was all for touch and go and we made it. Within minutes Harmattan had engulfed the city and we were stuck for 7 days there as other flights were not coming due to poor visibility. These incidents in my flying career reminded me that there power above, which helps you have faith. From Accra to Rio-De-Janerio is only 3 hours and 30 minutes flight, across the pacific. {"ACCRA HAS ITS OWN BEAUTY BUT POOR COUNTRY, PEOPLE ARE FRIENDLY AND GENTLE"}.

CHAPTER – 4

SINGAPORE

I have had many experiences on flights to Singapore. First of all, I must mention that this is a former British colony. Singapore considered a contemporary, commercial cosmopolitan city state. This being a multination of Chinese, Malaysian and Indian settlers which adds to its complexities. It is a diverse nation full of color and flavors worth enjoying.

There are certain do's and don'ts in every country while visitng and travelers must obscure those. Singapore also has many, such as chewing gum, import or possession can invite trouble as spitting is an offence and can earn you a hefty fine. Two, In toilets, don't forget to flush, this is a courtesy expected and offense can earn fine also. Three, nudity is not tolerated. Four, no littering is tolerated either as the city is cleanest in its reputation. Five, never rest your feet on the table or even point it towards others as it considered against etiquettes and so is patting on the head as this is considered to be sacred. During discussions never bring up religion and politics, these are considered sensitive issues and termed offensive. Tourists may enjoy taxi rides but their Mass Rapid Transit (MRT) Bus System is cheaper, comfortable, convenient and rather affordable. In mass transport buses, it is not considered friendly to munch eatables. Tapping in to unsecured WiFi is considered a crime, almost like hacking or misusing a computer. Always find a secure and a known WiFi connection to log into. Tipping is not a standard cultural practice. In some establishments, service charge is added in the bill. So is in Japan, tipping is not appreciated. It is important to know that gifting must be done carefully as gifts should never be wrapped in white color wrappers. Never gift clocks, handkerchiefs or flowers as somehow these are all associated with funerals. Alcohol offered to Muslim Malay or Indian Singaporeans or even pig skin gifts must be avoided.

Gifts should not be opened openly in front of the giver but in privacy. Don't smoke in public it is prohibited. The knowledge of the aforementioned points is rather informative to a tourist in this multicultural society. Make sure to avoid drugs, considered a serious crime. Pointing a middle finger at someone is considered rude. It is always helpful to know the Do's and Don'ts of your destination cities. I learnt from my Singaporean friend during my stopovers in Singapore and mentioned here to my readers, who may find it informative.

Places to visit for a Tourist:-

Singapore Zoo, Flyer, Botanic Gardens, Universal Studios, Jurong Bird Park, Marina Bay, Merlin Park, Sentosa Island, one can go by ferry or Cable cars and enjoy the view all around to Santosa island. and last but not the least Little India - here one can really enjoy the vibrancy of Singapore's Indian culture. You can be easily immersed into the smells and tastes of the aromatic food in the range of various Indian restaurants. South Indian dishes are very popular, also here try bargaining shopping. Little India has its own charm for the visitors.

Marina Bay Sands:-

Opulent Marina Bay Sands is a resort. The complex includes Hotel, High end luxury brands, a mall, and even a canal running through. One can visit the observation deck on top of the hotel, grab a snack and watch the impressive skyline from the roof top restaurant.

Singapore Flyer:-

World's largest giant observation wheel, one can see he view of spice islands of Indonesia, Malaysian straits of Johor.

Botanic Gardens:-

Is definitely worth a visit some parts of the park are very beautiful when lighted at night. Good resturants to enjoy dinner. It is very big park at the end of orchard Rd. Most of the locations, I might have forgoten as New development have taken place. Last, I visited as a tourist a few years ago and was surprised to see, the big changes in Singapore. I feel, it is a must see country. In late seventies, while flying for Air India, I was posted in Perth in Austrralia and regular flights from Perth to Singapore, with two/three days stay, gave me enough time to explore this beautiful country.

China Town:-

Authentic Chinese food served under bright red lanterns, all excitement in this distinct. One can enjoy the Chinese heritage culture. Another temple worth visiting is Buddha Tooth Relic Temple.

It is fascinating to learn about the birth of Singapore. It is said that Sir Stamford Raffles had stopped here in 1819. He saw a small fishing village and its potential as a Port so he purchased the land from the Sultan of Johor and invited Chinese and Indian migrants to move there. These were the seeds of multi-ethnic identity of Singaporeans.

Santosa Island:-

… and its underwater Aquarium world is a must for tourists.

One can even swim with the dolphins. Another must see on Santosa Island is Merlion.

It has a head of a Lion and body of a Fish. Lot many water sports at the warehouse. It is highly recommended to visit the Santosa Island in a cable car as it is the most enjoyable. Last time, on my visit as tourist a few years ago, I found santosa filled with excitement. One can visit Universal studios, movie themed zones, filled with rides and outdoor shows visiting the world`s largest Aquarium, with more than 100000 marine animals, leopards sharks and giant octopuses, adventure cove. If have time, one can stay in one of the resorts there enjoy excellent meals.

ESPLANADE PARK:-

HISTORY OF INDIAN NATIONAL ARMY: (Subhash Chandra Bose)

This was set up in the South East Asia with Japanese help in the year of 1942. They encouraged and even forced Indian soldiers to form INA to liberate Indians from the British. The monument stands within Esplanade Park, dedicated to the unknown soldiers from INA.

There is so much to enjoy in Singapore for the tourists. In fact, this small country is considered to be the cleanest in administration and economically steady and multicultural without any prejudice against each other. People are very peaceful and business-minded. I was impressed with Singapore's tourists needs such as wheelchair facilities, visually or hearing impairments and security in the public amenities.

FEW THINGS FOR TOURISTS TO REMEMBER

Never discuss, religion, Politics. Never sit with pointing your feet towards others, never Give gifts in white wrapper to any one , never open the gifts immediately received from some one infront of him. Tourists should avoid littering, throwing cigrettettes and trash no tipping smoking drinking in public is prohibited. Dont eat or drink at a station or inside the train. Dont chew gum. Drugs are strictly not allowed and punshiable. No crazy parties or loud family dinners after 10 pm. In short must respect the local laws. It is the safest place for tourists even at night. Tourists visiting religious places, temples, fine dinning, clubs, wearing shorts are not allowed. Spitting in public is strictly not allowed. Never point your index finger, it is considered rude. One has to be cautious of these things never give hankerchiefs, clocks or flowers as these are considered connected to funerals. Never give gifts with your left hand but with both hands to pass the gift.

Never give gifts of alchol or things of leather to a muslim. Never carve names on public park beches it is punishable as, destroying or damaging public property it can create big problem. Getting angry, raising your voice, physically fighting just not tolerable in law. There are many temples to visit. one of the famous one is sri Senpaga temple devoted to Lord Ganesha. In fact In Sanskrit, Singapore means "Lion City."

There is very famous and beautiful temple, "Sri Krishna Temple" another worth visiting is the oldest temple sri veera naha kaliamman temple, one of the grandest and oldest Hindu temple, dedicated to Goddess MA KALI

CHAPTER – 5

PERTH- Western Australia

It is the 4th largest populated city in Australia. It is located on the river swan coastal plain narrow strip between Indian ocean and Darling scarp. This town has the largest mining operation center and large business houses. While I was flying for Air India between Perth and Singapore, I was posted here for 2 months and enjoyed the Australian culture and its multi-ethnic community. In fact, it is called the land of immigrants. Influx of immigrants after the World War-II. Predominantly from Britain, Greece, Italy and Yugoslavia led to the rapid population growth. In the late 20th and the early 21st century, the economic growth flowing from several mining booms. In fact, its port of Fremantle served as base for submarines operating in the Pacific Ocean. Australians are lively people, fond of outdoor life, watersports, etc. Originally, the people called 'Abrogins' were the real natives but later on the British established it a convict supported settlement. I had visited many Australian friends, who showed me very proudly the old photographs of their forefathers, who had come there as convicts.

Life in Perth is pretty laid back, relaxed and easy going. Cruise in the river Swan and a visit to Darling Harbour are very interesting. Visit to its Botanical Garden and the Zoo, cruising in the Swan river were simply amazing. Also had the chance to visit the Bell Tower, one of the largest musical instruments in the world, located in the heart of the city. The night life here is not as vibrant as experienced in Sydney so let's fly to Sydney and see what's in store for my readers.

AUTRALIA IS A SMALL CONTINENT WITH FEW BIG TOWNS ON THE PERIPHERIES AND IN BETWEEN ALL DESERT IN THE North STARTING WITH DARWIN THEN COME DOWN IN THE WEST IS PERTH THEN MOVE ALONG TOWORDS EAST COMES ADELAIDE THE MELBOURNE AND LITTLE ABOVE IN THE EAST ON THE PEREPHERY COMES SYDNEY ABOVE COMES CAPITOL CANBERRA. WHEN THE TRUCKERS CARRYING GOODS FROM THE EAST COAST TO THE WEST, A DISTANCE OF ABOUT 4000 KMS TAKING THEM ABOUT 45 HRS THROUGH THE DESERT. IT IS VERY LONG JOURNEY SO IN CASE ANY HELP IS REQUIRED, AFTER SOME DISTANCE STOPS ARE MADE IN BETWEEN CALLED REPORTING POINTS. FROM THERE ALL INFORMATION IS REACHED ABOUT THE POSITIONS OF TRUCKERS. THEIR TRUCKS ARE DESIGNED WITH AIRCONDITIONED CABINS, SMALL KITCHENETS AND SLEEPING BERTHS ETC. HELP CAN REACH BY HELICOPTERS PEOPLE CAN TRAVEL BY, AIR FLIGHTS EVERY WHERE IN AUSTRALIA. FEW YRS. BACK HEARD AUSTRALIAN GOVT. WAS PLANNING INTER LINE RAIL SYSTEM SYDNEY VIA MELBOURNE ADELAIDE TO PERTH. AS WE KNOW AUSTRALIA IS DOWN SOUTH OF EQUATOR SO THEY HAVE SUMMER, WHEN UP NORTH WE HAVE WINTER AND VICE VERSA, THEREFORE LOTS OF TOURISM FROM EUROPE TO AUSTRALIA DURING WINTER AND SAME DURING SUMMER AUSTRALIANS TRAVEL FROM SOUTH TO NORTH. IT IS WORTH AND ENJOYABLE A VISIT TO SYDNEY AND MELBOURNE, TENNIS AND CRICKET TOURNAMENTS ARE QUITE FAMOUS. TENNIS CHAMPION SHIP IN MELBOURNE IS AS FAMOUS AS WIMBLEDON. I MUST MENTION HERE, NEWZELAND, AN OTHER BEAUTIFUL COUNTRY IN THE SOUTH PACIFIC. NEWZELAND.

FROM AUSTRALIA TO NEWZELAND IS ABOUT2200 Kms. BUT SHORTEST IS FROM THE SOUTHEREN TIP OF TASMANIA TO NEWZELAND ISLANDS IS ABOUT 1500 KMS. WHEN DURING MY POSTING IN AUSTRALIA WHILE FLYING FOR AIR INDIA, I USED TO MEET MANY INDIANS SETTLED IN NEWZELAND, WHICH IS IN THE SOUTH PACIFIC. I WAS TOLD, IT WAS VERY SCENIC AND PEACEFUL COUNTRY AND INDIANS SETTLED SPECIALLY IN THE CAPITOL WELLINGTON HAD NO PROBLEMS, JOBS HOUSING ETC. IT IS VERY DEVELOPED COUNTRY, NATURALLY EXPENSES IN CITY CAPITOL ARE LIKELY TO BE HIGH BUT I WAS TOLD THAT SALARIES ARE ALSO GOOD. THOSE INDIANS I HAD MET WERE QUITE COMFORTABLE THERE.

SYDNEY:-FAMOUS OPERA HOUSE

As we prepare to land in Sydney, on approach, we are greeted by Australia's iconic performing Arts venue- the Sydney Opera. It is a multi-performing Arts centre in Sydney. It was opened by the Queen Elizabeth-II on the 20th October, 1973. Very well-organized opera tours give an insight how this marvelous building looks. It is very important to enjoy one of the performances in the theatre. Many concerts take place. Orchestra performances are really impressive. Good restaurants, souvenir shops and walk around and watch the harbor bridge with Botanical Gardens located on the right- side which waits to be captured on your cameras.

Sydney's opera house is listed under World's heritage site by the UNESCO. A graceful building shaped like a shell. It has a magnificent structure with walkable guided tours available.

Most memorable day was enjoying new year eve, when fire works start from this bridge. It so happened that I was on temporary posting in sydney for air india flights sydney to singapore and back, from my hotel window, I could watch this beautiful fireworks. Actually the new year starts from australia. I was very fortunate to watch new year eve celebrations in three countries during my air india flights. 2ND time in paris from hilton near the eiffel tower and third time in new york [in times square].

Sydney Harbour Bridge:-

It is of an utmost pleasure to walk and enjoy the harbor carrying all rail, vehicles, cycles, and pedestrians. This bridge also goes by the name of 'Coat-Hanger' for its design. It was opened in the year of 1932- on the New Year's Eve, most beautiful colorful fireworks show is a treat to watch as the New Year begins right here in the world.

Bondi Beach:-

Most popular beach is located just 7kms east if Sydney and regular buses operate here. Surfing, water sports and swimming in the sea are very popular but strictly between red and yellow flags and the complicity guarded by the life guards. Floating on the surf-boards is very popular. It's a paradise for sun bathers, separate areas for nudists to sun bathe. During summers, the sunrise from the ocean is at 4:30am and is really eye-catching. Bondi beach has a main shopping centre in Hall Street having large numbers of Beach wears, hats and sunglasses.

Many cafes with home style cooking and many coffee-shops. There are few night clubs for the young and many bars.

Taronga Zoo:-
… in Sydney is an unforgettable sight to visit. It is only 12 minutes from the city by the mode of ferry. From here on, one can enjoy breathtaking views by Sydney Harbour. Koala Bears and other 4000+ animals- one can take a tour, children enjoy the playful Koala Bears. There are many shows, events and concerts held. There is plenty happening at Taronga Zoo. Children enjoy the fun with baby elephants, pygmy hippos, jumping kangaroos and many more, especially jumping kangaroos with babies in their pouches who are very friendly towards the kids. Kangaroos and Koalas are on the of the list for children to have fun.

The Rocks:-
It was historic where the Aboriginal people lived and later the convicts pitched their tents. One must visit The Rocks Discovery Museum which narrates their history from Aboriginal folks to convicts and tourist spot through their art galleries and market stalls. I still am not able to experience the night time ghost tours.

Circular Quay:-
… is a ferry terminal for Mandy , Watson Bay and Taronga Park Zoo. In the annual winter, one can witness the migrating whales, watering cruises takes the passengers out to view these magnificent animals. Darling harbor is situated on a walking distance, a water-front Pedestrians precinct, full of shops, Restaurants, musical entertainment venues. One can enjoy another Madamme Tussads, Sea life Sydney aquarium. It contains world's largest Australian Marine creatures- something to remember. Lots to enjoy for the children and 'carousals' for the young, water parks, Jet boat rides, Racing car adventures, and other attractions. Families can have a fun day.

Sydney Tower:-
It is soaring in the city's skyline at a height of about 309 meters, city's tallest building at city's busy centre which is Victoria Point shopping mall. Lifts take visitors to the skywalk - made of glass floor viewing platform. A panoramic view having a revolving restaurant to grab a quick meal. Here I experienced meeting a Sikh gentleman running an Indian food station with wife and sister on the ground floor shopping mall. I must admit that we both were delighted with a small chat in 'punjabi' language. Enjoyed punjabi food, praathas with chicken and other delicious dishes.

Many shopping malls on Pitts street and the Strand Arcade near George Street. It was a short walk from The Hilton, where I was staying. A day out at Sydney cricket ground where Australia was playing against New Zealand cricket match. Very enjoyable afternoon sipping chilled beer and enjoying the crowd gathered for the match.

Sydney's Hydepark:-

Amidst the bustling crowd and office people, this is a nice shady picnic spot, flowers, fountains, a central park, specially city workers come during break to relax and enjoy their packed lunches in the shade. As many Chinese are, immigrants here, so a beautiful eye-catching China town also has to be there. It is popular for authentic Asian cuisine. On the first full moon after 21st of January, these streets come alive during celebration of Chinese New Year feast with dim sum, Vietnamese photo Teppanyaki. Here as usual, bargaining is a must for the tourists shopping.

Sydney has may hotels to suit one; ranging from budget to 5 stars to mid-level. For the first-time visitors, tours and public transport is highly recommended. Hop on and hop off buses are very well connected. This stops at major sights in the city centre.

A great experience to go on a Sydney whale watching cruises. Tourists get enthusiastic to take a day's trip to the Blue mountain's nature and wild life.

I was on a temporary posting as a 747 Captain from for Air India to Sydney for about 10 weeks, flying Sydney-Singapore sector and had the privilege to enjoy all this in Australia. One thing, I would like to mention here that some of my readers should know the Australian OPALS are quite famous specially black opal for the ladies jewellary, not very expensive, nice gift for your wife/girl friend.

Now, it's time to leave this continent and fly to Europe with my readers.

CHAPTER – 6

GERMANY

I have some interesting incidents remembered and still miss my lovely stay in Frankfurt. Air India flights from Delhi to Frankfurt were looked forward by me. The reason being that was doing my first 747 flight to Frankfurt from Delhi as a Commander we took off in the morning and the Aerial route took us through the part of Pakistan then over the mountains Across over to Uzbekistan between Tashkent and then cross in to Ukraine near Capital Kiev, leaving Moscow on the right about 40 minutes of flight and then turn left in to Southern part of Poland on to Frankfurt in Germany. Well after crossing the mountains I lost an engine being my first solo I asked the flight engineer to check the fuel as we shall have to descend from 3,500 to 3,100 ft. to maintain the flight.

Now, I had to keep in mind, for the emergency landing in case another engine loses power. It was risky to cross the mountain again back to go to Pakistan. CAPTAINS OF ANY AIRLINE MUST, CONSIDER IN CASE OF EMERGENCY NEVER TRY TO TURN BACK CROSSING OVER THE MOUNTAINS AS ANOTHER ENGINE MAY FAIL THEN WITH TWO ENGINES THE POWER WILL NOT BE ENOUGH AND IT WILL RESULT IN A CRASH IN THE MOUNTAINS.

So I alerted Tashkent to be ready in any eventuality but things went fine with the aircraft and continued to cruise at 31,000 ft. though fuel consumption had slightly increased then entered Ukraine and alerted them to be ready as well as Moscow in case of diversion. Crossed into Poland, Frankfurt too was informed to give priority landing on arrival. What an experience, in short all went off well and safely landed on 3 engines in Frankfurt.

FRANKFURT IN GERMANY,

During my flights to Fanfurt, I used to have a Lay over of three days. During my lay over, there were many places to visit. I found that Hotel desk at Reception can be good guides to recommend places to see of tourist interest. Apart from other places they recommended RAYAN VALLEY RIVER CRUISE. They only booked it for me for pick up and drop back. Every thing was beautifully arranged. I was picked up in the morning and taken to the harbour, where the passengers boarding was done and slowly this ship started. on the open deck as it was cruising, the English speaking guide kept her commentary explains all the old castles on the bank of the river and their history and importance in olden days. The trip lasts for about 2 hrs or more, then at one place it stops near the bank and passengers who wish the castle for 15 mts are deboarded and taken for a quick tour so much of German history is revealed, so knowledgeable. Really, i was amazed. Well then the cruise ship returns and passengers are put in their buses to return to the hotels. There is so much to enjoy even underground metros, lots of eating cafés, Restaurants etc one can get any thing as during winter in cold, it is the best place to go underground for different eateries.

OCTOBER FEST

This festival starts in late September to early October its a very big beer festival.actually it is mostly in Munich,Bavaria Frankfurt and other important towns,some thing to enjoy where all streets in Frankfurt are full in front of all restaurants.there are tents pitched, seating tables for groups and large beer mugs with beer are ordered.friends book the tables sit together and enjoy. It ends till first Sunday of October. I happened to be there and enjoyed watching the German crowds enjoying singing and all fun.Tourist really enjoy the sight and if Happened to visit then must attend this fun in Germany,May be in Mun ich, I was surprised as during my flights flying over Munich,ATC users to name Munich as MUNSHAN.Firstly I was confused but later understood ,MUNSHAN is same as MUNICH. Another thing for tourist to know that OCT 3rd is a National Holiday in GERMANY as it is called GERMAN UNITY DAY like our INIPENDENCE DAY. IT IS GERMAN UNIFICATION DAY.Really missed visiting BERLIN to watch the famous BRANDUNBURGGATE. IT WAS FAMOUS FOR EAST GERMANY AND WEST GERMANY. IT STANDS FOR GERMAN UNITY AND FREEDOM. Its reunification was done on Dec 22 1989 since then its very important for tourist who hap;pen to visit Berlin to visit and get themselves photographed in front.Well there is so much,in summer months to enjoy in their gardens,cafés etc but only problem comes sometimes the language barrier bt now no problem every one understands and speaks English.Germans are very fond of beer and German sausages,every bar restaurants serve on order.Well,as I said i used to do many flights to Frankfurt then Halt of couple of Days then Fly to Paris.Those were really GOLDEN DAYS inAIRINDIA MAHARAJA AIR LINE.ONE REALLY INTERESTING INCIDENT,MOST INTERESTING INCIDENT FOR READERS OF THIS BOOK TO ENJOY AND LAUGH,WELL,IDEA IS TO MAKE MY READERS OF THIS BOOK TO BE GLUED TO READING TILL THE END AND ENJOY, { KADI PAKOREWALI}........... ENJOYABLE INCIDENT.

Kadi Pakode Wali

Wise people first think then speak, if it's vice-versa, it brings agony, pain and regret, as it cannot be reversed later. That's why God placed the brain above everything in the body. After brain come the eyes and the ears, nose and then tongue in the proper usage.

On one of my flights to Frankfurt, I was staying in Marriot Hotel, a few kilometers away from Kaiserstrade, the main shopping avenue. It was cold and snowing in the afternoon. After a couple of beers in the bar, I got a strong urge for Indian food. Myself and other crewmembers decided to go to Kaiserstrade beating the cold, to visit an Indian Sardarji's restaurant. All dishes on display were mouthwatering. I spotted piping hot kadi (Punjabi style).

"Sardarji is this kadi pakode wali," I enquired politely. Sardarji looked at me venomously and thundered, "Can kadi be without pakodas" "yes Sir. Sindhi, Gujarati kadi are without pakodas," I replied with a sheepish smile. "Then why did you come here; you should have gone to Gujarat," he said, with a disdainful look in his eyes. Wisdom prevailed and I quietly ordered kadi and rice. While eating, I observed a young Punjabi girl, dressed up in red Punjabi suit, jewelry, seemed newly married, talking to Sardarji smilingly. She seemed to be his daughter.

Next morning, I was doing Air-India shuttle flight to Paris and back to Frankfurt, and same flight was to proceed to Delhi at Air-India departure counter. Third day, again we decided to visit Sardarji for lunch. "Sardarji, the young newly married girl, who was here day before, was your daughter who left by Air-India yesterday," I triggered Sardarji. With the same ferocious look in his eyes, he barked, "who the hell are you"

"I am a commander of Air-India and flew the same aircraft yesterday from Paris and I saw her leaving by that flight to India." "Oh, Sahebji, why didn't you tell me earlier, these Air-India Staff were very rude and charged her 300 marks for extra baggage," he said with an apologetic look." "Sardarji if you were little polite to me day before and wouldn't have advised me to go to Gujarat for the kadi, I would have saved your 300 marks" after my meal, he simply refused to charge me. I hope he learnt to use his brain first and then the tongue.

Capt. S.M Mehra

Air-India Jt Gen. Mgr.

One day during our stay in Frankfurt,after few drinks in our hotel we decided to go to a Sikh Punjabi restaurant on KAISARSTRADE, ONLY TWO KMS FROM OUR HOTEL MARRIOT BUT THE BUS STAND WAS INFRONT OF THE HOTEL.Well i found a Sikh gentle man in his late fifties. I found among the dishes displayed at the counter was a Punjabi KADI so I asked" sardarji is this kadi Pakore wali,He looked at me with a sneer and said,Is there any Kadi Without Pakoras,I said yes in Gujarat and Sindhi Kadi, in India,so he said why you came here go there to eat Kadi. I kept quiet and we paid the bill,then i found a young Punjabi girl coming and clinging to her father looked newly married with red bangles.Any way next day i brought my flight from Paris,A quickSHUTTLE, returncflight.On landing I found the same Sardar ji s daughter arguing with check in departure counter staff for paying extra for baggage,.Next afternoon we crew members visited same Sikh restaurant for Lunch,I asked Sardar ji yesterday your daughter left for India,he looked at me. I said i saw her at airport,Sardarji said yes But who are you,I said I am Air India Commander,OH BHAPAJI MAAF KARNA,she had to pay lot of money for her baggage to AIR INDIA,I smiled and said," sardarji,If two days back,If you did not say go to Gujarat to eat Kadi,Then yesterday i would have asked counter staff not to charge,he looked at me,. SARDAJI profusely apologised and refused to charge the bill for our Lunch.I laughed and paid him,just remember don't be rude to your customers, and we walked away.This incident was published in Pioneer newspaper in Lucknow in India.

STOCKHOM_SWEDEN

On one of my flights to Fanfurt, I was asked by cousin brother settled in STOCKHOM. He insisted that i must visit him. I managed to get a complimentary return tkt by Lufthansa airlines to STOCKHOM. Plus my local AI manager accompanied me to get me VISA for SWEDEN So i left Frankfurt early morning and reached Stockhome, picked by my brother and stayed there for one day. He took me around the beautiful places in his car and showed as much, he could but the most exciting visit was to the place where NOBLE PRIZE IN DIFFERENT CATOGARIES IS FINALISED BY THE COMMITEE.

Really it was so memorable and worth my visit. Well, next day returned to Frankfurt to take my Air India flight back to Delhi. Short visit to SWEDEN but really worth it.

CHAPTER – 7

SWITZERLAND

Switzerland has always been on high priority of the travelers because it carries imaginary Picture of Paradise on earth with its scenic surroundings in the minds of the people. It is a rich people's playground. Now, it has become more accessible to the mid-income, who have more spending income. Lot of package tours are organized for groups which are well within budgetary limits. Air India had regular flights via Rome to Geneva but without any stopovers.

I always enjoyed the sight of its Fountain in Lake Geneva or the Alpine Lake, jetting water up to 140 meters high is a real eye catcher and while approaching to Land, From the cockpit, one catches the sight of this, also called 'Jet De Eau' in French. Travelers enjoy taking 'selfies' with its background. It shoots 500 liters of water every second at a speed of 200 km/hour, making it the city's famous landmark. The promenade around the lake with its beautiful gardens and fountains and not to miss itsFLORAL CLOCK {picture enclosed}, Boat cruises are very pleasurable in the Lake. Infact half of of the lake is in French area. Travelers always want to visit Mont Blanc as well. Again, it is better to get in to guided tours by Coach with a guide. The Coach travels through the splendor of the Swiss.

Country side to Chamonix, a picturesque Alpine town and from here ascend to the Aiguille Du Midi, a peak in a cable- car and from this peak, one captures sweeping vistas of the French, Italian and Swiss Alps on their cameras. Here one finds good restaurants to rest and grab a snack, etc. One can view the Peak of Mont Blanc, a little further, where Air India Boeing with famous Dr. Homi Jehangir Bhabha had crashed in 1961. I visited on private holidays three times for more than a week each time as I had a very good friend who was an executive indian working in ILO HQRS. He was a great host and showed many sites of Many UN Hqrs based there. BANKING THERE is in Complete trust between the Bank and depositor. It is the basic principle of free banking system. Now, I am told some agreements are made between GOVTS and Banks to check money laundering. In Geneva. WE Visited Hqrs. Of RED CROSS , W.H.O.ILO Etc., he was living alone in a beautiful apartment in a posh locality and invited me many times. He was also my guide to show me the beautiful sights in Switzerland, From Geneva, He drove me to Zurich, a real great drive to to see country`s lakes and mountains, it takes you through the heart of Switzerland. Once he took me via bern-lousanne route and returned via lake Geneva route. Infact Zurich has more busy district with famous World re- knowned Banks and big industrial hqrs i was told by my friend that there are 450banks in Switzerland and spl. Zurich only half a dozen are engaged in retail banking, rest are involved in wholesale trade and world invest ments. Banking system is kept in complete secrecy devoid of any Govt interference. Bern is the capital of Switzerland. As a tourist, I found cruise in lake Geneva, very enjoyable and one must not miss visiting flower clock, it is an outdoor flower clock in western side of jardin anglais park. I was told about 6500 flowering plants and shrubs are used [picture enclosed] The second point of interest is a scenic railway ride to mountaineers, home of Mer De Glace, the most famous glacier in France. Here, the tourists can view the magnificent work of the Artists who have crafted different things only on ice, and even rooms with furniture, etc {Another like this is in sopporo}.

This shall be mentioned in my Chapter on Japan, visit to the Sapporo where an exhibition is held annually during December. Same Exposition of Many World Heritage Monuments Crafted in Ice. {In sopporo} After this visit which is all inclusive in the package tour from Geneva, one heads back in the evening. This Chamonix guided tour is worth every penny. Visit to Mont Blanc. It is the highest mountain in Europe at abot 15 700 feet one can go by cable car fromChamonix, it takes you to Aiguille Du Midi about 12700 feet then change over to another cable car to reach the top. There are few Cafes. here the breathing becomes heavy as low exygen, one must keep water bottles etc. Many viewing decks are there for beautiful scenic views from the top.

Same way one can come down by cable cars. To base at Chamonix. It is better to visit during Summer as in Winter, its freezing cold up there. Many, young folks, I saw Skiing down. It is a life time Experience in Switzerland. I Had the opportunity to visit twice on a holiday, once with my wife and second time alone. Both times Visited MONT BLANC.

LAKE CRUISE:-

There is no better way to experience Geneva Lake than a narrated boat tour. There are dinner cruises also. One can enjoy the scenery around the Lake from the boat. The dinner or the meals offered at the cruise are plenty with good sit-in service and an enjoyable cruise.

EVIAN-LES-BAINS SPA:-

I was very impressed with a tour to this place. Classic spa town on the shores of Lake Geneva, Evian water of different varieties to cure different diseases, comes from different taps and it is mentioned which tap for cures a particular disease. There are cures available for Digestive, Metabolic or Rheumatic problems.

All treatments are depended on water. Evian water comes from the Mountains surrounding the area and endorsed by the Health Ministry of France. This center is famous for Health Fitness.

HOTEL MANAGEMENT SCHOOL:-

Swiss high-quality Hospitality education is famous for its flawless academic teaching. Swiss practical training and breath-taking scenery, offers bachelors and master's degrees in Hotel, Tourism, Events and other Management courses. It is regarded in high order by the international chains of hotels like Hilton, Marriott, Hyatt and the like.

ZURICH:-

This city in Switzerland is a Global center for banking and finance in the world. It lies on the north end of Lake Zurich in Northern Switzerland. The river Limmat flows through the centre of town with both sides of it, one finds famous banking offices. This city is known as an economic and cultural metropolis. Here, I learnt that about 450 banking offices are there and banking branches but only few dozens do retail banking, others are for trading. The high light of these banks are that all banking business is kept most confidential without any Govt. interference but now I believe some GOVTS have some agreements with Swiss Govt to be able to check on that to avoid Money Laundering.

One can visit Lausanne, a French speaking town on the shores of Lake Geneva and also can visit Bern which is the capital city of Switzerland. This is the city considered with best quality of life.

Some of the Swiss laws can really amuse a visitor. Sunday is considered to be a 'quiet day.' No loud noise of any kind, lawn mowing, washing of car or clothes to hang out to dry; all of this is considered offensive.

THE HQRS. Of WHO and ILO of the United Nations are in Geneva whereas the Main headquarter is in New York, U.S.A. UNESCO has its offices in Paris, inaugurated in 1958. These two headquarters in Geneva employs around 2,700 officials from over 150 nations and 40 field officers around the world.

Annual international conference in Geneva is held in June and laws are formulated concerning Labour are then crafted and adopted. {pictures enclosed] From a tourist point of view, Switzerland is one of the top destinations with easy accessibility. One can always taste and enjoy the best of chocolates (swiss chocolates) and watches around the world are famous. Chocolates like Coop, Woolworths, Minor, Lindt, Toblerone, Munz, Ragusa, and ever popular Nestle. Even at the Geneva Airport one can collect these chocolates as gifts for near and dear ones. Some of the liquor chocolates are heavenly and one enjoys the lingering taste for a long time. Another famous one are with fruit dipped in chocolate, a truffle, fudge or other sinfully delicious treat.

CHAPTER – 8

HOLLAND

Well after Murano, we decided to have a walk through the narrow streets with shops bustling of tourists. It was time to return for our flight back to Rome. My readers must know that this is all from the flashback of 30 years for a light read and to enjoy the dream flight with the writer himself.

AMSTERDAM:-

This is the capital of Netherlands. There are many things for the tourists like Rijksmuseum - the national museum of diamond cutting factory.

Real knowledge of the city can be grasped and experienced by the city walk. The guided tours help to understand the rich history this place has to offer and takes you to the best places, even to enjoy the night life. Some people like a Bike Tour which is a popular mode of transportation by its people. The Canal Cruise in Amsterdam is famous . Then hop on and hop off Bus services are available or a romantic candle light dinner available on the cruise itself these evening cruises are always every where, are famous for its dinner on board, which are more romantic and tourists love it.

VONDELPARK:-

... is a very popular one especially during the spring and summer seasons. Where people would love to enjoy sunshine and relax. Locals prefer this to be a family picnic spot on holidays and Sundays.

RIJKSMUSEUM:-

This features over 8,000 exhibitions of work of art. It is the most popular museum, I loved looking at Rembrandt's and Van Gogh's paintings. Vermeer and other Dutch famous masters of art. And also vast historical artifacts paintings of other masters shows the history of the Dutch culture.

ANNE FRANK's HOUSE:-

It is better to take a guided tour, this is where Anne Frank and her family hid during German occupation by the Nazies. during world war-II. The guide explained the Secret Annexe where Anne Frank had hidden and wrote all this for more 2 years. The door way that led to the Annexe was hidden by a marble bookcase. Those who worked in that building during that period supplied Anne and other with food and supplies. On August 4th 1944, this hiding place was discovered and all inhabitants were deported to concentration camps.

Only Otto, Frank Anne's father survived. Later after the war, when he returned to Amsterdam he got all papers and diary of Anne Frank. Now this house is a protected place like a monument for visitors to see for themselves. Even a Hollywood movie was made on this, "Anne Frank's diary."

All the horrors of German-Nazis and cruelty to the Jews were depicted. For tourist, it is highly recommended to visit this place.

AUCTION OF FLOWERS FOR EXPORT EVERY MORNING:-TULIPS

It is something unbelievable, The Flora- Holland flower auction in Aalsmeer near Amsterdam and Schipol Airport is the largest market in the world. I was told that about 20 million flowers are traded here. We took a guide, who took us very early in the morning to observe this function but from a walkaway from many meters above the flowers in warehouse. Mini transportation trains going in a crisscross direction in this world's largest covered market. Millions of flowers are traded annually. Flowers arrive around 10pm and cooled and sorted out at night, to prepare the cartons for auction in the morning. Visitors watch behind sound proof windows. Trading is done electronically. Huge screens show display auction information. By the time its afternoon, all flowers are cleared. These boxes immediately transported to Schipol Airport loaded in planes waiting and flown all they are put in shops in London, Paris and other places around the world. Day trips to this Aalsmeer may be taken by the tourists if the time permits.

TRIP TO KONKENOFF:-

… Another flowery paradise on earth. My visit to this place reminded of flower beds in Shalimar Gardens in Srinagar, Kashmir, India.[Tulips are grown in SRINAGAR also at a smaller scale] I would strongly recommend a visit to see the beautiful colourful tulip beds in rows after rows. A Bollywood movie "Silsila" was also filmed here many years ago.[Photograph is enclosed for the readers to experience as if they were with me to these Tulip gardens]

Konkenoff Park is located in south Holland in a small town of Lisse. Coach tour is the most comfortable from Amsterdam approximately 7 million flower bulbs are planted annually which covers almost 79 acres. Most beautiful Spring Gardens, about 800 varieties of Tulips bloom. The best time to visit this place is in the month of April. Gorgeous views of blooming Dutch Tulips and other flowers for which Holland is famous for. This is the most beautiful Park in the world as per my knowledge. This place is very close to 'Hague'[IN DUTCH CALLED "HUG', the international court of Justice by UNO (United Nations Organization). It is only half hour drive. On return journey the coach stops there for 20 minutes for the visitors so that they can take pictures and rest. Now our next stop of our coach journey is Madurodam.

MADURODAM:-

It is a miniature city depicting Holland. Top tourist attraction, it's a replica of famous Dutch landmarks cities and development. Here one feels so excited like a kid. It is open all year around. I was so thrilled to see the replica of Big Ships passing through Canals. A lock and dam system enable large ships to move by raising the water levels by this system. It makes the river and canal waterways more navigable. Same system was installed in the Panama Canal, waterway between Atlantic and the Pacific, ships travel through a waterway by this system of Locks. This is the same depiction in this Madurodam Park.

After this, coach moves towards Amsterdam via the Coastal Road, giving a beautiful view of the beaches full of crowds enjoying the North Sea. On the way, the coach stops at THE WORLD FAMOUS INTERNATIONAL COURT OF JUSTICE, tourist can take pictures. As mentioned earlier.

DAM SQUARE:-

… Situated in Amsterdam, it is a tourist attraction- at night many night clubs, DJ's, techno clubs, glitzy spots where one can spend the whole night. At the backside, there are many 'Love-Ins' where beautiful girls sit behind the glass inviting customers which reminded me of Bkk Nights . It is better to take a tour for the night life to enjoy the best what Holland can offer.

Dam Square is a town Square in Amsterdam. It is close by walk form the Central Station and near Damrak, a wide boulevard lined with Souvenir shops, trains criss-crossing, and bustling with tourists. Holland has its own Madame Tussauds, fantastic view of Dutch pop culture, models of Queen Beatrix to DJ Tiesto and national celebrities, these are all close to Dam Square. In the end, I shall emphasise that visitors must experience a Canal Tour, passing by Monumental Architecture, loop around the Historic Centre, and the open top boat is more enjoyable during the seasons of Summer and Spring.

ROTTERDAM:-

Is a major Port City in the Dutch province of South Holland. Maritime Museums and vintage ships exhibiting seafaring their lorries. One can experience inner city Canal System, largest port in Europe. Harbor cruise is very enjoyable indeed. Hop on-Hop off buses are available throughout.

One thing a tourist must watch from avoid tripping of thieves, keep your cameras, documents safe with you. Don't immediately trust people approaching you, or scammers with sad sobbing stories to scavenge money. Though this goes in all countries but as a rule be careful. Rotterdam has more of drugs activity especially walking at night.

It has the busiest port in Europe with most efficient Cargo handling. Overall, if time is short one can omit a visit here to proceed from Amsterdam itself. Rotterdam is only 87 kms from Amsterdam and coach tours are available throughout.

CHAPTER – 9

ITALY

In my travel experience, I personally felt, In Europe, Italy has much more to offer for the tourists. So much roman history is displayed on it monuments and other interests.

So let's fly to Rome:

After landing at Fumichino Airport, Rome, one feels the good sunny climate, with smiling faces and a friendly atmosphere.

Their rhythmic accent to speak in Italian with lots of hand gestures are noticeable. For sight-seeing, there are plenty of tours and English-speaking guides. In fact, one can enjoy leisurely walk through fashionable via Veneto and via Nazionale-heading to via Vasto.

The tourists venture out to famous Colosseum with lot of Roman history and Gladiators. The name 'colossal' means its size, it is about 500 meters in diameter and was inaugurated in A.D. 50. It depicts the gory battles between Gladiators, slaves, wild animals, Prisoners in combination. This was a kind of entertainment for people and Roman rulers. It could seat around 5,000 spectators.

Who cannot forget the famous and popular Trevi Fountain where millions of visitors have dropped coins to fulfil their wishes. It is a fantastic work of Art and much more than a mere sculpture. The streets around this square are bustling with tourists and vendors. One wonders at the turbulent spring that seems to flow out of the ground. It is an extraordinary sight with light and shade effect. It is a real fun to enjoy the sight of people, couples, youngsters and lovers, throwing coins over their shoulders and wising for good luck. The history tells an ancient legend that a young Roman girl showed the source of water from the spring to thirsty soldiers. 'Trevi' derives from the name of area, meaning three streets. Though it is attributed to the famous 'Bernini' but most of the part of the Roman architecture, is attributed by Nicola Salvi. I am sure many readers who have seen the famous movie, "We Dolce Vita-By Fellini" with alluring Anita Ekberg, who jumps into this fountain with clothes on and invites the famous actor Marcello Mastroianni.

TIVOLI GARDENS:-

One can take a day trip this is again listed under World Heritage list by UNESCO. Impressive fountains, nymphs, Grottoes playing music from the water fountains. The whole landscape depicts ruins of ancient villas like Villa Adriana. Waterfalls and an aqueduct tunneling beneath the city, shows the engineering skill of the Romans.

HOW THE POPE IS ELECTED:-

Popes are chosen by the College of Cardinals Conclave when the apostolic seat falls vacant, Amongst the Cardinals, the Pope is elected by majority of Cardinals. When the conclave is in session, it is held in a closed room, there is black smoke coming through the chimney outside. The existence chapel showing that the Conclave has still not come to a final decision. When the smoke or "Fumata Bianca" flows out of the chimney, then the world knows that a new Pope has been chosen by the Conclave. This chimney is placed atop the Sistine Chapel. Then the crowd gathered in St. Peters square outside gets jubilant. And finally, it is announced to the world, who would be the new Pope.

SISTINE CHAPEL:-

This is the official residence of the Pope in the Vatican City. Approximately 25,000 people a day come to visit this. It is famous for its Michelangelo's fresco. The ceiling in this Sistine Chapel was painted by Michelangelo between 1508-1512 with breathtaking paintings. This is the most famous work of Michelangelo, it is so memorable that the visitors just marvel at the sight. I was taken by a spell, looking at a painting depicting the birth of Adam, as a part of a series of biblical frescos on the ceiling of Sistine Chapel.

One needs a full day to be spent in Sistine Chapel alone. The most noteworthy things that the visitors would surely enjoy are the paintings by Michelangelo, which shows the portrayal of 'God' as a muscular figure with hair and big white beard as we can imagine. This was the first time God was depicted in this dynamic way earlier. It was depicted simply as a hand reaching down through the clouds. These frescos can be seen from 300 interactive images. Other frescos paintings depict "the last judgement," "forbidden fruit Vatican has its own Swiss guards and its own stamps. These guards are recruited from Switzerland's four Catholic Cantons to protect the Paintings and protect theVatican, is the smallest country in the world.

VISIT TO PISA (The Leaning Tower):-

This is the city of Pisa, not far from Rome. One can catch a train from Termini, the central railway station to reach there. The Leaning Tower is a free-standing Bell Tower. It is only 186 ft tall but has achieved worldwide recognition. This was built in the 14th century resulted in 14500 ton Leaning Tower in PISA.. The only mistake was the foundation was made on the dense section of clay. The foundation was only 3 meters deep. They clay was not strong enough to hold the tower upright so the height of the tower tilted. In 1964, the Italian government needed help to prevent the Tower from toppling because of its importance and tourist attractions. The engineers came together and with a temporary measure, a laden counter weight approximately 800 tons was installed and in 1987 it was declared a UNESCO world heritage site. Now it is sturdy and safe. Climbing the tower is the most popular tourist activity.

Here, on my visit, I was told an amusing story about an American tourist, when he parked his rental car near the tower one Italian agent came with his notebook and asked him to pay 10,000 Liras and gave him a paper in Italian. The visitor thought it to be a parking receipt and paid 10,000 liras. Later on, he got the note translated and found that the agent insured his car, in case the Lean Tower fell on it. What an innovative way to make money.

TRIP TO CAPRI AND BLUE GROTTO:-

Capri is an island in Bay of Naples. It is famous for the rich and famous with its upscale hotels, shopping and designer fashions of handmade sandals. It is famous for its natural Blue Grotto, a dark Cave where the sea glows electric blue as a result of sunlight passing through the cave at a particular angle and gives the water a blue color inside, the entrance to the cave is narrow and only for 4 to 5 boats enter one by one inside the magical tinge of Blue give its magical view. Blue water over the white sand underneath a blue glow in the cave, cave is big enough tourist really feel mesmerised. One should reach Capri by the mode of ferries which departs from Naples and Sorrento.

This Blue Gratto is 60 meters long and 25 meters wide and the cave mouth is only 2 meters wide but only 1 meter in height whereas the depth is 150 meters. Which is the reason why upon entering the cave the visitors have to bend slightly and go there in small row boats with 4 passengers max. It is so magical to enter the cave and enjoy the bluish color all around even when water is taken in hand looks blue. After visiting the Blue Gratto, visitors can take a bus to Anna Capri on top where the beautiful Tower is located for Lunch, snacks, etc. I visited three times during my Flying days. Second and third time through Kayani tours, a conducted tour. It is really a Rich people`s paradise, who have built residential properties in Anna Capri. CAPRI——FAMOUS BLUE GROTTO.

I still remember, trip to Capri and Grattos I had booked through Kayani Tours, very close to via nationale and termini station. It was a package with coach tour to Naples, then ferry to Blue Gratto followed by a bus to Anna Capri for lunch and then finally to a ferry boat back to Sorrento. In Sorrento you can find the same coach with English speaking guide, tour though the beautiful city of Sorrento All the roads lines where beautiful orange trees were so colorful, and back to Rome, on the way stop, for dinner at one of the many restaurants situated all over the place. And lastly drop at night to the hotel, enjoying all inclusive, an enjoyable and memorable trip. On the way from Sorrento, the English-speaking guide pointed out Mount Vesuvius near. MOUNT VESUVIUS is famous for its Eruption.

POMPEII:-

Now, I am told there are many such coach tours by other companies to cater to tourists. The cost of such packages also has risen ten folds in a span of 25 years. Here, I am taking only my readers through flashback memories of 30-35 years ago.

Mount Vesuvius is on the southern coast of Italy. It is the only active volcano on main land Europe, known for its volcanic eruptions in A.D. 79. The world remembers that on te 24th of August, A.D. 79 this Mount Vesuvius near city of Pompeii erupted, within the next 25 hours. It had wiped out the entire town. Hundreds of years later, archaeologists excavated Pompeii and found everything and everyone had been there, perfectly preserved in the volcanic ash. Pompeii is only 90 miles south of Rome. After this memorable, educative trip the coach dropped us off at our Hotel Holiday Inn at night after dinner en-route.

TRIP TO VENICE:-

Venice is always a dream for the lovers and honeymooners. Pictures of Gondolas and the oarsman serenading with Mandolin sailing slowly in the Canals and the lovers holding hands and looking into each other eyes, promising to be together till eternity. Venice is about 500 kms from Rome. One can drive it down which might take about 6 hours or so. Or can rather opt for a train or even go by air. Train from Rome covers this distance in about 3 hours and 30 minutes.

On this flight I had taken my two children along. I thought of taking them to Venice. They would enjoy more than going to Florence. So, I approached ALITALIA AIRLINES in Rome, if I could get interline, complimentary tickets to Venice and back the same day in the evening. Fortunately, we managed and three of s left the next morning for Venice. This is built on more than 180 small islands in a lagoon in the Adriatic Sea.

It has no roads just canals including grand canal and under the famous RIALTO bridge, through which, all the water taxis ply. One can take this water taxi from the airport as well. So I decided to take this public transport of water, but chose the one taking a longer route to the main St. Mark's Square which can give us a longer trip, going through canals under the bridges.

It was very fascinating drifting through the Grand Canal and watching water front Palazzos, Palaces, Churches and so much more. It was a dream ride watching the Gondolas passing by and people waving from atop the bridges. After alighting at St. Mark's Square, we visited the St. Mark's Basilica, which is filled with Byzantine Mosaics and the Bell Tower offering views of the city red roofs. I must mention the Rialto Bridge, it is the oldest bridge across the Canal and most popular for the tourists photo session on it. This bridge crosses over the narrowest point of Grand Canal and the heart of Venice. Since, we had to fly back in the evening to Rome so couldn't spare time to visit other marvels in architecture but had lunch at one of the open road side restaurants in St. Mark's Square and headed for the Ferry Station for a visit to the famous Islands of MURANO and BURANO.

ISLAND OF MURANO:-

This was very educative to learn the art of healing- fine sand, sodium, calcium and few other minerals and rolling it into the glass. A guided tour helped us in explaining the process. We were then taken to a room, where hot burning furnaces were shown with the expert glass blowers making the molten glass into artifacts, vases, pieces for shining chandeliers and other beautiful art pieces. One has to be careful while there, shopping spree, as you can find the exact similar things for a lesser price in st Mark`s square, but most probably from Murano glass factories where one can definitely find cheaper imports as compared to the far east. Even, some notorious oarsmen get the tourists on their boats in the name of Murano but take them to other Island where fakes are made and make them purchase it, thinking it to be real Venetian. My experience deterred me from purchases at Murano also, as for the name the items were priced steeply. Well that is Italy and one needs to be careful.

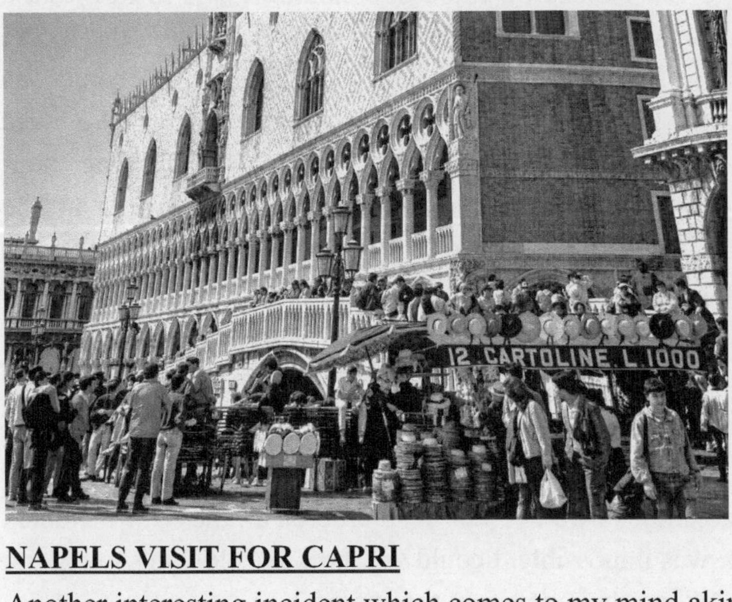

NAPELS VISIT FOR CAPRI

Another interesting incident which comes to my mind akin to this for the readers to enjoy with the insight. In Rome, on an earlier flight. My cockpit crew and I, totaling four;We wanted to visit island of CAPRI, so thought it would be cheaper to travel by train for Rome to NAPLES and by taxi to the shore and take a pax ferry boat to CAPRI for visit to its BLUE GROTTO, so after arriving in Naples, hired a taxi from the station for Naples sea shore where the Ferries operate to Capri , after reaching the taxi meter read 18,000 Lira so I paid the amount to the driver, then he asked others to pay the same amount individually. We were shocked when he said, "18,000 you, you, you and you." Can anyone believe this can happen in such a country? We called the policeman and complained, both spoke in Italian, then the policeman passed a smirk and told us that the driver was right. That was shocking and outrageous both of them were hand in glove, that was Italy for me.

SPECIAL SMALL CHAPTER OM MY EXPERIENCES OF DIVINE MIRACLES, MOST INTERESTING FOR MY READERS TO READ.

OUR DESTINY:-LET ME MENTION ABOUT MY DIVINE EXPERIENCES WITH DIVINE MIRACLES

"3 MIRACLES experienced that left a stamp on my life and made me to believe that there is a super power which controls us."

I would like to mention that miracles do happen and the blessed ones experience it. I couldn't have imagined two of them happened to me within seven days and that too, when my destination was Rome.

I. I cannot forget the first miracle happened when I was an Indian Air Force pilot flying as maritime Pilot based in Pune from 1958 till 1967. I was a young flying officer detailed with another sr. pilot, for a flight in B-24 Liberator 4 Engine 2nd world war bomber aircraft from Pune to Car Nicobar, a flight of 9 hours. It was to carry out a recce for an Indian naval cutter with 4 persons, reported to be missing in the Indian ocean since the past two days. The approximate position of the missing people was given to us by the naval control room in Maritime Hqrs in Mumbai. We were equipped with Maywest, floating jackets and parachutes; aircraft being non-pressurized though. When we were, flying above the sea about 550 miles from the Indian coast we lost power in No. 4 engine. we were flying at a height of about 8,000 ft and was unable to maintain the same and started losing height. Tried best to revive the power. At 5,000 ft sent a "Mayday" signal, with position, altitude, and intention. OUR, flight Egineer, had gone down the lowere deck where power generating equipment was placed for the engines, he found that particular engin fuse had blown for super charging the engine so he replaced that.

In the mean time, the altitude had come down to 3,000 ft so ordered all the crew members to bail out at 1500 ft as ditching, was impossible. I could see the waves looking so big but this was no time to feel the fear but to regain power in the engine.

At 1,500 ft the flight engineer got the engine power picked up to my relief. we started to the climb back while sweating and breathing heavily. After couple of moments had passed of heavy breathing the flt Engineer came up to the flight deck and told us , that the fuse in the engine super charger in that engine had blown. He managed to replace it in no time and regained the power. Well, the super power of almighty gave us another life. Proceeded to search and finally found the naval cutter in the sea. Flew one circle over them, passed their exact position to the naval maritime control room in Mumbai and further proceeded to Car Nicobar. Landed after a memorable flight of 11 hours. First thing after landing, literally I could sense God Almighty the devine power which saved us.. I walked away from the aircraft to light a cigarette and puffed heavily- looked up and thanked the almighty God. I was very young at that time only 23 years old flying officer was blessed with another life. (current age: 82 years old).

II. **<u>SECOND MIRACLE:-</u>** In 1989 I was flying a 747 as a Captain from Delhi to Rome. Early morning during the month of October our flight was scheduled with 249 passengers and 17 crew members with full fuel as the fuellers in Rome were on an indefinite strike and were advised by Air India Rome, to bring extra fuel for next leg of flight i.e. Rome/Geneva. As I lined up for take-off at Palam Airport (now known as Indira Gandhi International Airport) Runway no. 28, I asked permission for my take-off. Started rolling on the runway and aircraft picked up speed. The term V1 is the calculated speed with weigh of the aircraft, length of the runway available, so that rejection can be made before it safely before a/c takes off. But between V1 and V2 speed it is difficult and then lift off takes place. Everything is recorded in the cockpit flight recorder. Co-pilot monitors the speed and calls when is Captain is concentrating on takeoff runway but his ears glued to the calls. Suddenly, I saw halfway of the runway a flock of vultures sitting in the center of the runway. In a second, it was flashed to me the danger as the sound of roaring aircraft reaches, vultures would fly up and being heavy cannot fly above the Engines of a 747 aircraft so they would get ingested and certainly create a fire outbreak but the ears were glued to the calls of V1 and V2 Well the V2 call was not given yet.

No choice was left, but immediately rejected take off as power pulled back heard V2 after three seconds, sat on the brakes with full reverse thrust. One of the vultures hit the engine no. 3 badly and a fire alarm went on. There was nothing much to do but to concentrate only to stop the aircraft within the runway length. Fire extinguishers inside the engine, were used to put off the fire in the engine. In the meantime, the Delhi Air Control tower was calling to inform us that the wheels were on fire too. Just manage to bring the bring back the speed to 40 knots and veered off on the last taxi way before the end of the runway and stopped the aircraft. Fire- fighter were on the way rushing to put off the fire. Immediately ordered emergency doors to be opened on the left side because fire outbreak was on the right side. Through the door slides, many passengers were evacuated and then stopped as the ladders were brought in by the ground crew and the rest of the passengers were evacuated normally. I remember, my shirt was all wet and I was still calm, In my seat, until the hostess brought a glass of water and shook me to drink, as I reached the arrival hall at the delhi airport. With my crew, saw all those passengers applauding when I appeared. This was a news on TV channels and newspapers. (exhibit of the news in

Hindi paper is enclosed) I received commendation from the Air India director of operations and Director General (DGCA) who himself conducted the enquiery at the airport immediately.

Boeing people too commended for a fine performance and high degree of skill in performing at crucial point of flight. I was Cleared immediately for flying. This was the second miracle The God Almighty blessed me with his kindness.

एयर इंडिया के विमान
आग लगी

नई दिल्ली, 14 अक्टूबर (भाषा) एयर
के एक बोइंग विमान के एक इंजन में आग
इंदिरा गांधी अंतरराष्ट्रीय हवाई अड्डे पर आग
गई। इस कारण यह विमान उड़ान नहीं भर
यह विमान रोम जाने वाला था और इसमें विमान
चालक दल के 20 कर्मचारियों सहित 248 यात्री
सवार थे।

एयर इंडिया सूत्रों ने बताया कि एयर इंडिया के
विमान "त्रिमालय" के इंजिन नंबर चार में आग उस
समय आग लग गई जब यह विमान उड़ान भरने के
लिए रनवे पर था।

III. <u>THIRD MIRACLE:- "CANONIZATION WHEN SOME ONE PERFORMS 3 MIRACLES, THEN POPE PERFORMS THE RITUAL TO DECLARE THAT PERSON A SAINT, OUR MOTHER THERESA WAS DECLARED A SAINT PLEASE READ ALL THIS BELOW."</u>

I had flown Air India flight to Rome in October 1989. After landing I would have a habit of always going to pray in Vatican, so this time I had the chance to go to St. Peters Church. Though being a non-christian myself I believe praying to the God Almighty in all forms and religions and that respect should also be given to all. Therefore, tend to be at peace while praying in a Church or a Temple or a Gurudwara and if allowed even at a Mosque or a Darga, and without forgetting to follow their rules and rituals of their respective sacred places. As God is one and all human beings are created by him. This was a Saturday so in the evening over drinks, asked my co-pilot who was a catholic if he would accompany me to St. Peters next day, being a Sunday. He agreed so next morning both of us visited Vatican. I was surprised that St. peters square was completely empty, not a living soul. Very strange that on a Sunday, how can St. Peters square be empty. The huge doors of Basilica were closed. I couldn't believe my eyes, I wanted to know the reason and the mystery behind it. I asked my co-pilot to help me to push the huge and the gigantic Basilica doors a little- 'Ah', there was a light coming through the little crack, we pushed more and saw thousands of people gathered there with all lights blazing. I could not believe my eyes when pushing through the crowd reach closer, saw the Pope carrying out a ceremony called "Canonization"- when someone who's declared as a Saint, dies. We remember reading about it in the books but to witness the ceremony in person is no short of God's blessings and a miracle. I was standing hardly 100 feet, from the Pope in his full regalia with cardinals behind him in this ceremony. I was told later that saints are declared after proof of their carrying out, 3 miracles and at times it takes 100 years to declare someone a saint. Our Mother Teresa was recently declared a Saint. After the ceremony, I went to a corner in front of the statue of Jesus and slumped in the chair with eyes closed and prayed the almighty for his blessings.

ANOTHER UNBELIEVABLE INCIDENT.

It happened, While Visiting Lord Bala Ji`s Temple in TIRUPATI, In mid seventies, while flying for Air-India, I, along with group of three persons, quite religeos, decided to Visit TiruPathy for Bala Ji`s Darshan. In order to avoid the long ques, we decided to Buy special Darshan, short line by paying extra money in advance for that date. Those days there was no digital transfer, so from Mumbai, I sent a cheque by express delivery to the Main office, four days in advance. Still the confirmation had not come with a receipt but my friends insisted to fly down to Chennai and then to Tirupathy, thinking, money must have been recieved by the office there. On reaching there in the evening, to our horror, we were informed that money was not received and we had to join the long que for darshan, that would take five to six hours. It was not possible. I requested to meet the high priest but they refused to give me his address as he had retired for rest in his house nearby. Some how we managed the address. I opened the door, a bulky figure lying on the floor resting. I touched his feet, with folded hands narrated our problem. He seemed quite angry and fired me to get out of his house. Disappointed, I came out to my friends waiting outside and we walked back to the main entrance to the Bala ji`s temple. I told my friends to go to the office pay the extra money and buy spl entry tkts and sat on the steps with my head bowed down in my hands and prayed to Bala Ji for his blessings as we had to return to Mumbai without his Darshan as the Spl entry Tkt window was closed. Suddenly, I felt, some hand on my shoulder, Looked up, some gentleman looking at me and said," you want to have Balaji`s Darshan," I said yes but now, its not possible. He said," follow me." I called my friends who were little away to come fast. We followed him to the main entry door, people in the que were watching, no one stopped him and us. He took us right inside to the sanctum sanctorum, Where Bala Ji`s Idol was glittering. He said to me, now have the Darshan and asked the priests to follow full ritual. I bent down on the floor with my eyes closed in reverence the Diety infront of me. We had good darshan for ten minutes.People in the que had stopped and were watching us. Then he said," satisfied" I shook my head and thanked him profusely. Then I asked for his name." you need not know that" and he walked away. We hurried back to our rest house as we had to catch the afternoon flight next day, back to Mumbai from chennai. So many years have passed, in between I visited Tirupathy many times but that incident has imbibed in my head and found no answere to that. It is said, if you pray honestly to the almighty, infact he is within you as your Atma, He listens to you.

Another Incident Of Divine Power: GURUVAYUR

{I cannot forget, till today it is vividly in my thoughts, how this could happen. Long back, on my Mumbai-Trivandrum flight, we used to have a long lay over in Trivandrum. We were put up in a very beautiful Hotel on the Kovalam beach. Really worth Experiencing the beauty of this location on the beach. Once, while my crew were all in my room over drinks and we Thought of Visiting GURUVAYuR Famous temple but it was far north past Kochi. I had a good Malyali Friend, who was running Cab services. I called him to the hotel and meeting him Told him our desire to visit Guruvayur. He agreed to give two of his cabs but since it was too far to cover in one day, we were advised to have a stop over in Kochi [Then Cochin] on our way back. Next early morning, we left with my Crew. Well we reached Guruvayoor about in the early evening. Oh God this happened to be some auspicious day and hundreds of people were gathered there, No chance to go inside for Lord`s Darshan. We were very disappointed and my crew told me to leave for Kochi. I was very determined to have the Darshan, There, Few Elephants, were beautifully decorated with Lord Krishna`s Pratima and with Muscians and Drums, People had gathered.

To carry out Parkarma around the temple. I thought of approaching the Head Priest for help to have Darshan inside the sanctum. My crew had gone out and sitting in the cabs. The Head priest listened to me that I Being a pilot in airindia and had come all the way from Trivandrum and have to go back for my return flight. He simply told me, his inability, with this kind of crowd out side. He saw my face fell down with folded hands infront of him. He felt very sorry and told me to wait as the Procession of this crowd was starting With all the Pomp and show for Parikarma around the temple, That time he could take me inside when no one else was in sight. Wow, As the procession moved away from the Entry door of the sanctum, He led me in for only few minutes. I just cannot believe, I was all by myself infront of the Diety, With my eyes closed and tears flowing with folded hands, I prayed to the almighty for this exclusive Darshan of Lord Krishna, Avtar of Lord Vishnu. Then head priest smiled and asked me if I was satisfied. I touched his feet and Thanked him and came out before the crowd returned. When I came out my crew wondered what delayed me for 30 mts. I told them about my Darshan. They just could not believe this incident. I believe whole heartedly, If one has faith and determination, such miracles do happen. I always believe that ATMA IS PAMATMA, God is within you. He knows every thing what you think, do whether good or bad. He is omnipresent.

CHAPTER – 10

PARIS, FRANCE or GAY PAREE

The most sought-after place in the world, known as a global center for Fashion, Culture and Gastronomy. T he main landmark in the minds of people is its Eiffel Tower and river cruise in the Seine River. T his Eiffel Tower is 324 meters high and most visited by the tourists. Next on the tourist list in Paris is the "The Louvre Museum"- with vast collection, tourists are delighted to see the paintings of Mona Lisa- another gothic Notre-Dame cathedral on the bank of River Seine. During the river cruise one passes around it. I cannot forget the famous Hollywood movie, "Hunchback of Notre-Dame."

When the tourists visit the Eiffel Tower, from the top it is so picturesque to see the Trocadera Gardens below. The night life is most glamourous and worth the visit to Pigalle. I still remember in my times about 25 years ago, the most expensive and sought-after night clubs were the LIDO, IN LE PIGALLE AREA .THERE ARE MANY FAMOUS NIGHT CLUBS ARE SITUATED SPECIALLY MOULIN ROUGE, THIS THE MOST VISITED PLACE AT NIGHT BY TOURISTS TO ENJOY REAL PARIS Moulin Rouge is in Montmartre area and its cabaret with glass of champagne as well as the Crazy Horse Saloon. The shows at Moulin Rouge include the famous Doris Showgirls, mesmerized by a parade of bejeweled and feathered costumes

as dancers and acrobats perform among elaborate sets including a giant aquarium hanging swings with beautiful sets and lighting as well as musical score. I always considered the famous Cabarets and performances in Paris at night at the 'Le Lido' on the Champs-Élysées, most enjoyable and wonderful evening with top performers, but very expensive, during my times which was about 25 year ago. The entry charges were about 1,000 FF with a glass of champagne and seating was more expensive. This was the place for the rich people, but one visit was a must to taste the extravaganza.

Nowadays, I learnt that many city night tour packages are being offered to Tourists with river cruise on the Seine at night and dinner as well. On top of that, open bus tours of Paris around its monuments. Champs-Élysées is something to remember walking past Arc de Triumph, the mere thought of this fashionable avenue still makes me feel nostalgic.

I am told that shows at Lido with dinner costs somewhere about 300$ per person-Lido show itself costs about 85 euros. For the tourists running on a strict budget can visit the lobby, watch pictures in the lobby of the performers, admire and leave. Other lower scale performance of Caberats are available in 'Le Pigalle', FAMOUS ONE MOULIN ROUGE - Champs-Élysées is the most popular avenue in Pairs and tourists satisfy their quench to taste Paris by taking a leisurely walk around.

PARIS AIR SHOW. 1969 {CONCORD AIRPLANE WAS SHOWN FIRST TIME} FIRST SUPERSONIC PASSENGER AIRPLANE FOR TRANSATLANTIC FLIGHTS BY AIR FRANCE AND BRITISH AIRWAYS.

I can never forget, on one of my flights in Air force Days to Paris, in 1969. There was Paris Air show at le Bourget airport, where first supersonic passenger aircraft The CONCORD was on display. I remember it was 29 may,1969. this was a prototype. It was a sensational news of this first supersonic aircraft flying twice the speed of sound. My self and another pilot with me decided to visit this airshow and from paris where we were staying, it was quite far, so had to travel by local train to Le Bourget airport. It was thrilling experience to see this prototype from inside and its cockpit. Though inside was quite narrow and no engines fitted. Later it was used by French and British for its transatlantic flights, I Think in 1973. We had the experience to see other countries aircraft on display and lastly the Air display by different aircraft flying in different formations. Now ofcourse bigger, better and more durable Passenger Aircraft have come but the memories of seeing the first passenger supersonic aircraft physically remains as a grand opportunity.

I visited Paris many a times, during my Indian Air Force days and later on as well when I was with Air India. Of course, in IAF days I used to fly military super constellation aircraft on courier duties from India with stopovers in Beirut, Paris and London and same route back or sometimes via Cairo-Paris-London.

I used to stay in moderate hotels with my crew in 'Place De La Concorde', it was almost end of Champs-Élysées. This was an obelisk erected in The Square, this was 3300 years old Egyptian from Luxor. There were many hotels around it and convenient to walk down to famous gallery 'Lafayette' with the famous biggest department store also located. This place De La Concorde looks beautiful with two decorative fountains in center of the square. There is history behind about the French Revolution Louis XVI and Marie Antoinette assassination. So, the present name is given to this square to forget about the past. People take pictures with these fountains, which again has a lot of history behind, about Egypt and Ramses II and III, tourists only enjoy the photo sessions there.

STUDENTS STRIKE IN IN FRANCE MAY 1968.

I was operating Air Force Courier Flight via Paris to London in May 1968, I cannot forget getting stuck during that one week in Paris, staying in a small hotel near Pigalle area, During that period due to students protests for many reasons with the French Govt. the whole country had come to stand still. That time it was Gen. Charles DE Gaualle as the President of France and complete chaos by students strike, I along with my crew were stuck and all food joints restaurants closed, we went through lot of difficulties. Ultimately the Owners of that small hotel, provided us meals from their own kitchen. Once the strike was over, we were instructed to return from Paris itself to India. These are memories of my flying career with Air Force and Air India. I really cannot believe that I some how had the misfortune of getting stuck in many countries during their political upheavals. As i had mentioned in previous chapters that got stuck in IRAN during Khomeini take over from the Shah of Iran, in ACCRA and other places well these memories become more interesting for the readers of this book.

Well tourists never tire to probe more and move in Paris. One of my flights, an interesting incident worth remembering as many readers may take a hint to move around in a crowded city like Paris to hail a Taxi for short distance. I was flying for The Indian Air Force in the year of 1965, during a courier flight from India to Paris and London to bring military spares for its hardware in a Super Constellation 4-Engine Aircraft.

My daughter at home was only 2 years old and fond of toys about cars. I called up my wife from London and spoke to the little one also. Upon asking her what she would like from London, she replied, "A Ferrari Car." I was amused how the devil can a two-year-old know about it? Now where to get a toy Ferrari Car, big enough for her to sit? Someone suggested to look for in Gallery Lafayette, Paris as they have a whole floor dedicated to toys. Since, I was leaving London the next day so no time was left to find it in London. On reaching Paris, after checking-in the hotel my flight engineer and I left for the Gallery Lafayette nearby, close to Place De La Concorde, where our hotel was. We found beautiful white color open top Ferrari to peddle down made for the kids. Without wasting much time, I bought one but the carton was quite large to carry on foot to the hotel so tried getting a taxi but no one agreed for such a short distance to the Hotel.

Then, I told one of taxi drivers that we were going to the Orly Airport, those days Orly was the International Paris Airport, Charles De Gaulle airport was built later on. He agreed, so I put the carton of Ferrari in the Car's trunk and told him first take us to our hotel nearby, pickup baggage then we'll go to the Airport. So, he brought us to the Hotel, I told him I needed to check with the Hotel's reception of my flight booking was confirmed. The driver agreed to wait, in 5 minutes when I returned I told him, "Sorry flight booking is not confirmed." Apologized and paid him 18 francs, as per the meter and tipped him 10 francs Thanked my God for this brainwave.

Such interesting incidents make the travelers more knowledgeable to find solutions in other countries. Paris is a city full of life, sidewalk cafes, restaurants, night clubs and a lot to enjoy in sight seeing. I once landed there with Air India flight on 31st of December, 1989, New Year in Paris is something to remember. We were checked in Hotel Hilton which was very close to the Eiffel Tower. I had taken my daughter who was only 16 years old that time. It was very cold and she being more sensitive to cold, preferred to stay in the hotel, my room, where the balcony was facing the Eiffel Tower so we both sat on this balcony after dinner to enjoy myself with glass of champagne, courtesy of the Hotel Manager and saw Parisians singing and dancing in the street below. Hundreds of them going up the Eiffel Tower, which was all lit up with colour and music all around. Though in the later years, I watched the same type of people merry making on New Year's Eve with splendid fireworks in Sydney from their Sydney Harbor Bridge but here in Paris the air was more romantic, full of fun, people hugging each other as in the Times Square, New York. I consider that each and every day like this is by the blessings of God, worth remembering. New Year celeberations in Times Square New york too happened on one of my Air India flights. We were staying in Lexington Hotel on LEXINGTON eve not far from Times square, so visited at night, to watch the people, new year, hugging singing dancing. really worth remembering.

New Year day was celebrated in Paris, next morning with a river cruise in Seine then lunch at Champs-Élysées restaurant and visit to the Louvre Museum. In the evening visited the famous night club Moulin Rouge with my crew. We enjoyed the 2 hours show with champagne and macrons. Here elegant attire is red and special VIP seats are reserved in the balcony, needless to mention, at a phenomenal price. The show was mind blowing, no photography was allowed in the show.

In this over-crowded theatre if one can afford VIP seats, is a real pleasure with champagne, etc at a phenominal cost..

You first cut the long time waiting and rather chaperoned to the waiting room to be seated in the balcony box, we could only enquire and bought normal tkts The VIP arrangement was for people, who could afford. The cabarets are out of the world, absolutely super and once in a life-time experience. There are packaged tours including the cruise, Eiffel Tower, and night clubs, hence, everything is arranged systematically. This reminded me of the movie made in 1952 with famous Jose Ferrer and the Hollywood sex-bomb Zsa Zsa Gabor, the Hungarian beauty. Visit to Nepolean Museaum was very informative. The most sought after dream of every tourist is to visit The Louvre, where People make beeline for Painting of Mona Lisa. It is a national Museaum anf most famous in the world. This a place to world`s most and extensive collection of art, from, many cultures. Most famous Leonordo da Vinci`s Painting MONA LISA, this painting has enegmatic expression, people ask, if painting was of a real lady well I was told by some friends there in paris that mona lisa in real life was a lady called Lisa Gherardini and wife of a Florentine merchant from Florentine. So many different stories but for tourist is only to see this famous painting inLouvre and get Photographed in front of this painting. In my times, it was allowed and people in line used to wait for their turn. Another one is Venus de Milo. Louvre is one of the largest Museums in the world, one cannot see all in one day. Napolean Museum is also in Louvre and history about Napoleon Bonaparte, He seized power after the great French revolution and after that people know his victories all over. For Tourists, it is not important with limited time and money, so better to visit famous places in Paris.

The most enjoyable in my case was cruise in River Seine and enjoy the ride under passing so many bridges. Specially at night time the cruise is thrilling, with Eiffel tower lit up and beauty of Notre dame, Lunch cruise or Dinner cruise is more expensive cheapest, I found was one hour round trip cruise from Eiffel tower, since Air india crew used to stay in Hilton near Eiffel tower so it was convinant. Transportation and guided tours are available for tourists. In my experience of travelling through so many countries, it was found to be more economical and informative to go for conducted tours, as to overcome different languages in different countries and selected places to visit. Well worth remembering Paris, the dream of every tourist.

CHAPTER – 11

EXPERIENCE OF MY VVIP FLIGHTS

FLIGHT CARRYING THE PRESIDENT OF INDIA, MOST MEMORABLE. {VVIP FLIGHTS, WITH INDIAN AND FOREIGN DIGNITARIES}.

GENEVA:-MY VVIP FLIGHT WITH PRESIDENT OF INDIA TO USA, VIA GENEVA, Late Gyani Zail Singh.

On the 6th of October 1982, I had the opportunity to operate a VVIP flight. This flight was from Delhi to Geneva with a VVIP onboard, the President of India, Late Giani Zail Singh will always be remembered as my most cherished flight, which changed my whole career in an upswing. I was considered the blue boy of VVIP flights. After this flight, where I was detailed to take the President for Houston in U.S.A. for his heart bypass surgery, brought me very close to the VVIP and he considered me and my family as a part of his family. We took off from Delhi after receiving the VVIP at VIP bay at Palam Airport, along with his elder brothers, daughter and son- in-law boarded with President's staff. The flight was normal and we landed in Geneva. The President and family were staying in a different hotel. In the evening, the local Air India Manager invited the crew to his house for dinner. As per the protocol, whenever the Indian Heads of State are passing a country, the stopover is avoided in the Capital Cities to avoid state

Flew late King Hussain of Jordon.He flew for a short time my aircraft from cockpit flying from Delhi to some places.Ambala Ahmedabad and Mumbai.he gave his autograph on this note as I could not find proper paper.

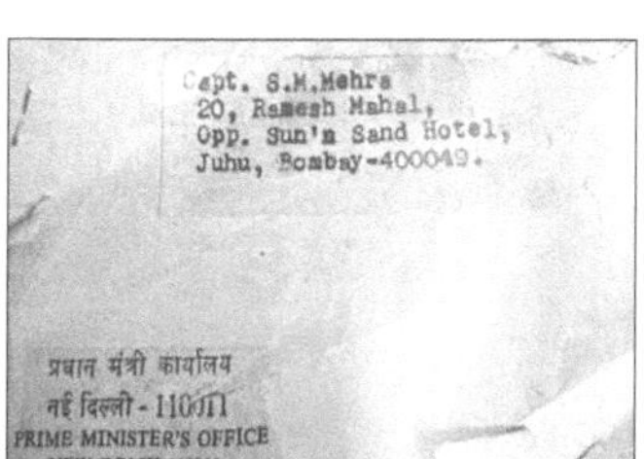

formalities as this being a private visit. At night, after dinner, when we returned to the Hotel, a message came from Air India Manager. That the President had a stroke so be ready for further instructions. The crew was alerted on standby. Till 3am, there was no news then the Manager called and informed that the VVIP was stable and prepare for morning takeoff for New York at 10am. So I got ready by 7am and with crew proceeded at 8am to prepare for the flight.

The President brought in an ambulance and boarded the special Air India's aircraft by a high lift and his bed was made with his personal doctor accompanying the President and we took off. After sometime, when overflying the Atlantic I paid a courtesy visit to the President. He was lying in his bed looked rested and smiled. So I sat nearby and told him about the flight and weather in New York and arrival time and wished him good health. He was very polite and smiling all the time. After landing in New York, I went back to check on him and sat with him for 10 minutes and he inquired about me and my family, etc. When I told him that a new Captain with fresh crew would take over to fly him to Houston he was surprised then asked me to come back to fly him from Houston after his surgery. I smiled and told that whomsoever Air India details, would come. He calls the Air India commercial Director U.S.A. who was present and told him to arrange for me to be detailed for his return flight. So I said goodbye to him and disembarked. Well, after 4 weeks, I was detailed to fly him back from Houston. He was very pleased to see me. He introduced me to his daughter and asked me to keep in touch. So flew him from Houston, Amsterdam and new crew took over. Those days the VVIPs used Boeing 707 Aircraft. I sent him the pictures taken on board the flight to President's house and he warmly reciprocated. This was the 'high' in my life of being a VVIP pilot in the Indian Air Force and Air India. Sweet reflections always bring a smile and a quiet whisper. 'Thank You God'!I cannot forget, another incident where I was detailed for a flight from London to delhi, It was normal flight and no body had mentioned about a special VIP flying on my flight, The great DALAI LAMA, after receiving noble peace prize on 10th dec 1989, he was travelling on my flight.

This great Budhist monk, whom, it is not possible to meet in india, even if one goes specialy to Dharamsala where he resides, next to impossible. After airborne from London, I decided to pay my respects in person and congratulate him about being awarded Noble peace Prize. So I went to him in First class, folded my hands and bent down near his feet. he blessed me with his hand on my head and smiled. I told him that I was very fortunate to get this chance of flying him. I could see the sparkle in his eyes. He said THANK YOU. As I said, these are some great incidents which an international flying capt treasures in his memories. {THESE VVIP FLIGHTS HAVE BEEN LIKE A CHERRY ON THE CAKE, LIKE MY READERS TO KNOW IT IS A GREAT RESPONSIBILITY GIVEN TO THE VVIP PILOT TO FLY SAFELY WITH CARE AND COMFORT FOR THE VVIP ON BOARD}.

CHAPTER – 12

MOSCOW

Delhi-Moscow-London and the same way back to have stop overs at Moscow. Well those days were with many government restrictions in Russia, moreover, the language barrier problems even on f lights entering Russian Airspace, the Air Controllers gave instructions in Russian language and we had an additional crew member as FRTO, like an interpreter to pass instructions to-and-fro. This made our conversation between Aircraft and the Air Traffic Controllers much easier.

Now of course, many changes have taken place, new hotels like Marriott and Hilton have come; people are more open to converse in English and new fashionable stores have opened up and modern restaurants with good music, etc. has made a huge impact which is pretty evident. During my times, we used to stay in a State-owned hotel with all Russian staff which was close to River Moscow and Hotel Rossiya.

GREAT RUSSIAN CIRCUS

I must mention a very interesting incident I had flown a flight from Delhi. After check-in at the reception, one of our hostesses came to me and mentioned the Great Russian Circus show in town was later in the evening and asked if we could get the tickets for the performance. That was a tall order. I smiled and told her looked difficult as it was on the last-moment but however, tired with the hotel reception. I was informed that all foreigners had to pay in foreign currency but now all shows were completely booked so there was no chance. By now, all the crew members had gathered around me. Well, what to do? So I thought of a novel idea- why not cash on Indian Sentiments, eh, "Hindi -

Russi-Bhai-Bhai" because the locals were heard at many places singing "awara hun" a Raj Kapoor's Bollywood film had earned much Bonhomie. So, I politely asked the ladies who were part of my crew to quickly change into their Indian Sarees but none of them had one. So, asked them to use Air India's uniform sarees and asked everyone to meet in 30 minutes in the lobby.

We were all set to try our luck at the circus. We quickly got in our taxis and reached the venue. All full, no chance but still hopeful to speak to the Manager there. He was a pleasant guy and heard me patiently that we an Indian crew only for 2 days of stay, anxious to see the Great Russian Circus and Artists. He showed his helplessness as there being not empty seats available. I again requested, "Sir can you allow us to sit on the steps in the Arena, we would be grateful as we otherwise will have to go back to India disappointed." He had no answers but agreed when I said 'Spasibu' (Спасибо) meaning 'Thank You.' He was highly amused, well, I had learnt few words, like 'how do you do, Good morning, thank you, etc.' in local language helped to get around in any country as an International flight Captain. Luckily, I had learnt basic Russian in Delhi University for few months which came in handy.

My crew was thrilled and I got them to sit on the steps without any cost. I am certain, my readers would like to use such interesting incidents during their travels. Always learn few words of the local language, especially the greeting ones. It is common way to greet anyone like 'Kakdela' or 'Kak Pazhivayesh' meaning 'How are You?' in Russian. It helps to break the ice. I had learnt that Captain of any International Carrier is not only good in flying but good to command his crew and keeps them happy and in a good humor too. Happy crew extends full support faithfully to their Captain and a happy safe flight can be conducted. Even after 24 years of retirement, my cabin crew members still meet me with love and respect.

In Moscow, there are many interesting places for sight-seeing. Moscow is on the bank of Moscova river. Kremlin is the power hub of Russia outside its red walls, is called the Red Square, Russia's symbolic center. Its home to Vladmir Lenin's Mausoleum and St. Basil's Cathedral, world famous for its colorful onion-shaped structure.

Let's start with Red Square and Kremlin Walls. One side is, once the site of the executions and military parades and on the other side, the largest Russian department store called, "The Gum." This store has everything one needs to look for. Then right on the other side of Red Square stands the famous St. Basil's Cathedral with colorful onion shape domes in Blue, Yellow, Red, Green colors; making it a central spot for photo sessions by the tourists. I always enjoyed the afternoon sunshine in Moscow, Gorky Park. This is the Central Park of culture and leisure with big water ponds and numerous fountains, situated amidst colorful flowers. Season of Summer is just amazingly beautiful here.

Another Park, which I enjoyed the most was 'Chistye Prudy.' It has a large lake; one can take a boat in the Summers or find people ice-skating during winters. Atmosphere is very friendly, one enjoys year around here. Botanical garden is another place to relax like in the Japanese Garden is made there.

METRO STATIONS:-

In Moscow, the metro stations are very attractive for tourists to enjoy and capture in their cameras. Metro system in Moscow is very convenient way of transportation. Engineering and artistic concept depicts so beautiful. It is such a relief to get in to a metro station when outside it is cold, snowing or raining. Good to travel on weekends when there is not much rush. During Summers, it is a pleasure to travel to different parks. Tourists need to be careful of the pick-pockets as they are in any other country. Moscow station is in the center so one can go in different directions. These metro stations are so decorative like a piece of art that one marvel at them. These metro stations underground was also safe from aerial attacks during the second world war. Moscow metro station being in the center, there are nine different metro lines to take travelers to different directions.

COSMONAUTS MUSEUM:-

This has always been on my priority list, whenever, I used to get time during my stay in Moscow on layovers, I made a point to pay a visit to this Memorial Museum of Cosmonauts. Here, one learns about wide variety of the Soviet and Russian space related exhibits and models which explore the history of flight, astronomy, space exploration and technology. It receives almost 300,000 visitors every year. I was thrilled to see the space capsule used by Yuri Gagarin, the first man in the world, who went into space I was very amused to learn, how YURI GAGARIN WAS SELECTED in fact the first flight in to the space the capsule which was sent in to the space could only fit in the astronaut up to 5 feet 7 inches and YURI GAGARIN was only 5'2' inches well that helped in his selection as the First human being in to the space though this capsule had only one circle around the earth and he was brought down with a parachute.. Soviet moon-rover is another interesting piece and one can find the manual from Apollo-Soyuz Test Report in Russian and English.

Though, I have been to Johanson Space Center in Houston three times, which of course is much more on a larger scale and more informative but visiting this museum truly shows the Russian's success story into the space.

OSTANKINO TOWER:-

It is another marvel to watch in Moscow city. It is currently the tallest free-standing structure in Europe and 11th tallest in the world at 1772 feet tall. This is marked for the 50th anniversary of Oct revolution. It is named after Ostankino, district of Moscow where it is located. This is a masterpiece of Russian Construction and Engineering skill. It is a T.V. and radio tower. This held the record for 9 years until Toronto, Canada's C.N. Tower was completed in 1976, which is taller by only 13 meters more. But it held the record as second tallest free-standing structure for 31 years, until Dubai's Burj Khalifa surpassed both C.N. Tower and this tower in 2007.

Tourists can enjoy the sight but I had difficulty on capturing this in my camera in a single frame, despite clicking it from a distance so got it in two frames, half-half joined the two pictures together.

BOLSHOI THEATRE MOSCOW "SWAN LAKE - CLASSICAL BALLET":-

It will be not fair to mention the most important Bolshoi.

Theatre in Moscow. This is an historic theatre with international fame. It holds performances of Ballets and Opera. It has a beautiful bar in the lobby. I was determined to visit and watch a performance. Number of flights during stopovers, I requested my friends for help. Once I was really surprised when an Indian Naval attaché in Moscow, a friend invited me for a performance, the most memorable, "Swan Lake," I can never forget about the climax sees the Power of True Love conquer the forces of Evil. The symphony orchestra was moving, enchanting and the stage management and lighting was just out of the world. The theatre surrounded by golden balconies with red curtains all around, gives a feeling of nostalgia as I write and I still can see that in my memory crystal clear to help me share it with my readers. Well, wanted to see Leningrad but there were no Air India flights to my dream place, restricted to Moscow only in Russia.

CHAPTER – 13

JAPAN

After long 40 years of my flying career with the Indian Air Force and the Air India, many delightful memories come out in the flashback. They are pleasant, informative and knowledgeable.

I thought of bringing them to my readers so that they can enjoy and relax. I wanted to bring them out which are imbibed and such rich experience should not go in vain in the sunset of my life. I have traveled or flown through fine continents in the world. I would like to take my readers with me on this dream flight starting from the far East, The Land of The Rising Sun, Japan and then slowly move Westward through other countries in Asia, Africa, Australia, Europe, and America.

Japan, this is an island nation in the Pacific Ocean with a lot of history. After the second world war the people of Japan had rebuilt their country and what amazing progress in construction, engineering and its culture. It always emphasized after the war, that Love, Peace, Harmony and Prosperity would endure in any country. Japan after the war, showed it powers in technology, manufacturing so much that its exports in electronics shook up the world and it became another advanced economic power and nuclear power for energy. Here I must mention, while visiting tokyo, tourist must not miss, visiting ginza, its most faboulous shopping stores area,latest items from dresses to electronics etc but specially for electronics, ons must visit akihabara shopping market, here latest electronic goods are in display.probably in my time I was shocked to see mini electronic mobile phones which probably came to india after 10 years so many electronic items like mini binaculars, cameras computers and what not. It was an experience to learn that japan was top most in electronics in the world.. So many items,i used to buy and bring home where people used to admire and keep asking more about japan.. This country has history going back many centuries of Imperial rule and still the King and Queen live in Royal Palaces but are historical heads of the Country and command high respect in the hearts of Japanese people.

I did many beautiful flights of Air India to Tokyo, Osaka and charter flights to Sapporo and Nagoya. Japan consists of many islands, four largest ones of them are; Honshu, Hokkaido, Shikoku and Kyushu. Their culture is ancient traditions blended with modern life. They are very mild, soft - spoken, etiquettes, and respect. I was surprised to see that tipping in this country is not appreciated. They have a high sense of self-respect. Who can forget their tea ceremonies till today- they like to keep their homes very neat, clean and peaceful as they strictly keep their footwear outside their house. Another thing which impressed me is that the Labor Force never go on strike to shut down their work but in agitation over work to show their frustration. Never seen in any country or anywhere else in the world. Now the government is encouraging people to work from home only if they want. Also, wants to reduce the long hours practiced in many Japanese firms and incentivize companies to switch paper for electronic devices. This is to help the working mothers to work from home. It was a treat to see Japanese so honest hard working, even women and with self respect. No tipping is permissible as it is considered not respectful well, from this one learns about the qualities they imbibe.

On my Air India flights to Narita, Tokyo we had a stop-over of 2/3 nights and it was real fun to venture out. There are many package tours with English speaking hostess guide.

Like trip to Mount Fuji and Hakone will take Ashi cruise with lunch, on return by the same luxury coach via old Hakone Town to get a feel of the small Japanese Houses hot springs and then taste of Bullet Train to Tokyo on return.

Tour to Imperial Palace Hiroshima Peace Memorial Park visit to beautiful Kyoto and Nagoya, etc.

During Christmas holidays, most of the workforce likes to charter and visit Buddhist Shrines in India. I was fortunate enough to do two such trips. I took a flight toSAPORO and other crew positioned there already brought the charter flight with more than 150 passengers in boeing 707 to India and I would stay with my crew for a week and on return of the flight would fly it back via Tokyo with normal load that way, i would explore these beatyful cities for 7 days.

SAPPORO:- {SCULPUTURES CARVED IN ICE AND MANY FAMOUS WORLD MONUMENTS DEPICTED CARVED IN ICE} MOST IOMPRESSIVE

This is the capital of Hokkaido since it was during Christmas and this being in North most of Japan experiences heavy snowfall and cold weather. It was fun to visit the city Square from the street down below, one could see the people skiing up there at the skiing resort called, 'Teine Ski Resort' the most memorable annual show of Snow Festival in Winter months January to February. Visitors and tourists flock here, main site is 'Odor' in Central Park, where an exhibition of Ice Sculptures is made and lit up during evenings. It gives a feeling of paradise, with castles, shrines and other sculptures carved out of ice. I was in Sapporo from December 24th to 31st in 1990. I cannot forget the cold, snow, ice on the roads but all enjoyable. It was Christmas Holiday Season so the Hotel had minimum staff but all acceptable and friendly.

MOUNT FUJI:-

I had taken my daughter on this Tokyo flight of Air India with three days layover so decided to take her on a package tour to Hakone, Mt. Fuji from Tokyo Central by a luxury A.C. coach with English speaking staff and on the way, saw the Great Buddha at Kamakura on way to Hakone {Picture enclosed}. We could not take the bus trip Mt. Fuji as it was covered with clouds, anyway, they took the tourists to 5th stage at 2,300 meters instead. So we elected to take a cruise after lunch there is Pristine Lake Ashi, after a long boat cruise for about 40 minutes. Went to Hot Springs and visited the old city of Hakone and returned by Bullet Train to Tokyo Central. Next day took a city tour visiting some Japanese Temples and Imperial Palace and proceeded to the famous Ginza.

Ginza is Tokyo's most famous upmarket shopping, dining, entertainment district. Famous department stores for shopping, art galleries and night clubs as well. It is full of neon lights during the evenings. It is like a shopping expedition of high scale fashion, art and mixture of old and new Japan. I was literally immersed in the five floors full of Japanese toys. There were about 200,000 items in that store, I was told about.

Dresses, women shoes, latest fashion handbags, and what not. Ladies really enjoy sometime going through these stores.

Hi-tech items, latest in the world market. There was Electronic street, where latest electronic items were for shopping. I could never had imagined that such items would be available in any other country.

DISNEYLAND IN TOKYO:-

One can travel by train there are so many attractions like Universal Studios. So many thrilling rides, splash Mountain, Theme Park, with different rides are quite enjoyable. This was the first Disney Park made outside the U.S.A. So many sights Disney's mickey mouse and other performances and performers in different attire of Disney ready for Tourists.

NAGOYA:-

Another charter flight of Air India was given to me for Nagoya, same way had the opportunity to stay there for 7 days and explore the city. Very beautiful, though Japanese are very reserved people but very humble. I requested my Air India manager to arrange a visit to Toyota Car manufacturing factory. This is the birth place of Toyota Cars. It is Japan's fourth largest city after Tokyo, Yokohama, Osaka and nations major economic center. Its G.D.P. tops many of the small countries. It is very cosmopolitan. Here, one must enjoy sushi, very famous restaurants to cater this.

Japan is country most advanced in Asia and one of the economic powers in the world. New generation is very hip and adventurous as well as highly fashionable but with old cultural ties. One thing, I noticed, they never invite any body home but take him to a Restaurant. Well, its own culture.

OSAKA:

It is the largest port city and commercial on the Japanese Island of Honshu. Known for modern architecture, hearty street food with some night life. Sumiyoshi-Taishais oldest and Shinto Shrine. I used to enjoy the sight of Mt. Fujiyama, or Mount FUJI, from the air when flying from Tokyo-Osaka-Sapporo route from the air as I enjoyed the flight from Addis Ababa to Nairobi and Saw Mt. Kenya enroute from the air as well as Mount Kilimanjaro on way to Dar es salam flight. . These are privileges of the Air Crew doing such flights to enjoy these sights from the air. I shall never forget my sighting once when Sun and Moon on the horizon were together early morning, flying from New York to London, so close to each other early morning. One was just rising and the other just appearing above the horizon. As a pilot such natural sights are very rare but to remember I had an occasion to stay two nights in Osaka and that too during spring time. The city was carpeted in pink cherry blossoms all over. Balmy night clubs above with stunning fireworks. It is the season to visit. In autumn spectacular shades of yellow, orange and red are seen as Maple Trees are ablaze in color.

Winter of course the city is covered with snow. In Osaka, I had purchased the different seasons Photogaphs from the Market [Pictures enclosed to see the SAESONAL beauty of Japan]This is the country where the sun rises first in the world. That's Why it is called "The Land of rising sun."

CHAPTER – 14

THAILAND AND HONG KONG

Air India had regular flights to Bangkok- Hong Kong-Tokyo. I visited this beautiful city of Bangkok many a times as a stopover for 2 days or 3 days.

This is a land of smiles, it was formerly known as Siam. The thai place are friendly for loving and it exotic and tropical climate and its Thai culture is very endearing for the tourists. In fact, this is the first locale, Indian tourists think of, its closer to India, affordable with a lot for tourists to enjoy its Golden Beaches, Gaudy Temples, water sports, cruises in the canals, floating markets and shopping. It has many malls for the shoppers and its famous 'Chatuchak' market where hundreds of stalls, sometimes 1500 hawkers sell all kinds of wares. Many conducted tours are available for sight-seeing. Canal tours, Temple tours, half day and full day tours. Another attraction is the Thai food which the tourists enjoy with Tangent, spicy taste. Temples like Golden Buddha, Emerald Buddha, Lying Buddha are a big attraction for the tourists (photos enclosed). Tour to Bangkok Palaya is quite affordable for the tourists, with now spending power among the working class, where working couples can manage a short leave together and enjoy such short tours.

Night life, well, night life with its night clubs and show girls with plenty of Bars are opened whole night to regale the tourists from all over the world. Its massage parlors are high on the itinerary of the tourists. Sukhumvit Road has plenty of night clubs, bars, thai city has to offer, not to mention the famous red light district of Soi Cowboy and Nana Plaza. All kinds of tourists are loitering and flirting with young hostesses. Well, this is one of the attractions for the tourists to taste.

One has to be careful as many young girls attired and skimpy dresses are in fact lady boys. One must enjoy thai boxing shows as well.

Pattaya, is the city on the Eastern Gulf Coast known for its beaches lined up with resorts and hotels, shopping malls, and 24 hours cabaret bars and 18 meters tall Golden Buddha. Big Golf courses and water sports are there to cater the needs of everyone. There are direct flight also but I along with my crew visited in a luxury coach which regularly leaves from Bangkok.

Its only 100 kms from Bangkok. We were very keen to visit its Crocodile farm and its underwater world. The crocodile farm show was a great hit among the tourists to see the stunts by the Thai. Performers puts his neck and hand in Crocodile mouth, etc. It all looked the crocodiles are heavily sedated for the show. Crocodiles in the pool are also an attraction to the tourists to offer chicken pieces through long sticks and the crocodiles jumps in water for the catch. Photo sessions for the tourists. The Million Years Stone Park and Horny Tigers for photoshoot, another attraction. Well, I felt that most of the animals were sedated for the tourists. The Stone Park is very nice and educative to see stones millions of years old. We did a trip by ferry boat to Coral Island from Pattaya, it was beautiful.

VISIT TO CORAL ISLAND FROM PATAYA: FAMOUS ALCAZAR NIGHT CLUB WHERE ALL TRANSGENDERS PLAY ON STAGE WITH BEAUTIFUL LIGHT EFFECTS. MUST VISIT PLACE.

It is a beach resort and most visited by the tourists to Bangkok and Palaya. A real treat for the beach combers and returns from Coral Island we decided to spend the night in PATAYA for its night life. Well, we were recommended to watch at 'Alcazar night club' where the entire show was conducted by most beautiful transgenders. One cannot believe they were not show girls but lady boys. The show and Cabarets were glittering with music and light effects. It was much more impressive than many night clubs in Europe. Actually, this show is different from the seedy side of Pattaya night life in the streets. After the show the performers meet the audience for a photo shoot for a small sum and when they talked in the manly voice we realized they were not women. Fantastic show and one should never miss it. After the show, we enjoyed dinner at an Indian restaurant and moved to the streets of Pattaya, for the seedy night life of the red light areas and full of Jugglers and road magicians enthralling the crowd. Well, next morning returned to Bangkok with its 'Tuk-Tuk' and traffic jams. This is all the tourists enjoy and tell their friends back home.

HONG KONG MY MOST ENJOYABLE STAY DURING MY AIRINDIA DAY.

It had many flights to Hong Kong from Bombay and Delhi via Bangkok enroute to Tokyo. In those days in late 1970s, we used to fly 707 Boeing aircraft on these routes. I still remember those days the airport was called 'Kai-Tak.' It is in the heart of the city. One side are the mountains on approach to the runway 13 and the other side was sea for runway 31. To land at runway 13, was little difficult as the approach started for landing from 8 miles but the runway was hidden behind the mountains so the pilot had to descend on the localizer of placed on the mountain keep descending and once reached 1 mile from the runway then through clearance of the mountain one could see the runway 13 to the right so the final turn to line up with runway for touch down was done. Descending turn and about 300 feet high one could straighten the aircraft in line for landing. It was considered one of the most difficult approach and landing in the world. The captain had to do a check flight under a check pilot or a flight instructor to be cleared as qualified. Runway 31 was clear and easy approach from the seaside. Now, of course, a new airport has been built little away from the city, located on the island of Chek Lap Kok. This is mainly, land reclaimed from sea. This is the fourth busiest airports in Asia. There are regular train services to this airport from Kowloon station.

It takes only 20 minutes to the airport. Regular bus services to Hong Kong Business Center and Harbor City are very convenient.

Hong Kong is a real treat and most popular with tourists for shopping and sightseeing. In my times in late seventies, it was a British colony with its English governor but still many Chinese were not fluent in English but after their Chinese govt. got back the state from the British, on my recent visit, found 100% population fluent in English and I was much delighted to visit its Disneyland. This Disney world, was second in Asia after Tokyo Disney world this is situated on Lantau Island, very beautiful. One needs two days to enjoy there. One can go there from Kawloon Bay via MTR [Mass travel Train from kawloon, or from HKG island by Bus or taxi, it is about 22 miles from there it takes about 30 mts. There are many Hotels in Disney world, one can stay there. From Kawloon, one can take famous Star Ferry to reach HKG island or Discovery Bay which has high value Residential and offices. From HKG One can go to Macau Island also by Jet ferry but needs a temporary Visa. Now I don't Know what are the Conditions since it has come under the Mail Land China. Another Important Tourist attraction is Victoria Peak which highest in HKG about 2000 ft altitude but there is very beautiful Peak Tram from HKG island to the top. From there one can have a Panararamic View of whole of HKG.. In seventies, on my flight to Hong Kong we had a layover for 2 days and stayed in Hotel Miramar situated on Nathans Road in Kowloon as it was much closer to Kai-Tak Airport. Now the aircrew stays on the other side on Hong Kong island. Miramar was a 5-star very good hotel, centrally located with shopping malls but always enjoyed its star ferry from the harbor to Hong Kong island making it a favorite and cheap transportation. The most enjoyable fiesta was Chinese New Year which comes in the mid-February. Fabulous parades and merry making Chimes, Dragons and other Chinese Pagodas, etc. on the floats in the parade. Gourmet food, music and light gave a real color of festivities. General holiday was being celebrated in Bank Offices, etc. but the restaurant industry was doing a roaring business. Almost 1,55,000 people including The locals enjoy the floats and 300 performers. Hong Kong is famous dragon floats during the Chinese festival.

LADIES MARKET IN KAWLOON.

Ladies market is famous on tung choi street, it was kind of cheap market to buy cloths etc run by ladies many chinese souvenirs were available to buy for home. Even children shirts, t shirts with some mickymouse printed. During my stays,i often used to vist and buy t shirts with my children`s name printed on them.they could do that in 5 mts infront of you.here you need to bargain, they are clever enough to know tourist. So haggling is necessary. I used to buy beautiful ladies pants etc for my wife and children.really loved to shop for home from there.

For tourist, there were quite moderate hotels in tsim sha t sui on the southern side near the victoria harbor in the by lanes, good markets places around and within tourist budgets.well now dont know as I visited last in 1995.

PEAK TRAM:-

Some of the other attractions for the tourists is a beautiful view of the glittering sky-scrapers, harbor and new territories from the top of the hill. This peak tram regularly departs from the ground to atop the hill. Not costly and tourists and families enjoy the ride in the tram going uphill. On top is the beautiful park and restaurant.

DISNEYLAND:-

This is another big attraction for the young, old and especially the children. It has MTR, [Mass travel Railway] This has all what other Disneylands in Japan has to offer, with theme parks, all the water rides and Disney Micky Mouse shows as well. Good restaurants to eat and take respite for a while. Beautiful castles and other enjoyable sights. It is a whole day outing for the tourists and families.

OCEAN PARK:-

Another big attraction is where they have a world-class aquarium where dolphins show, dancing and jumping for spectators is full of amusement. Thrilling rides and different shows and activities the avenue of Stars where most celebrities from Asian movie industry are mentioned in those stars. This ocean park was opened in 1977. It is a marine life theme park with thrilling rides and an amusement park. This ocean park is about 1.5 km long and has a cable car system, most convenient but has most scenic route and view of hkg and south china sea. During my service with Air india, I was posted there temporarily for Two weeks and had made many Indian friends, who were my guiding factor for all tourist places. Later they shifted to Discovery Bay and after retirement from Airindia, I had gone again to HKG to visit them so enjoyed their hospitality in Discovery Bay.

DISCOVERY BAY:-

It is up market residential area located on the Northeastern coast of Lantau Island in the new territories, great place to get away from the busy Kowloon. It is a serene development surrounded by South China Sea peaceful oasis from hectic Hong Kong. It is also closer to the Hong Kong International Airport, through a tunnel, oceanfront dining for memorable culinary cuisine. Surprisingly no petrol or diesel driven transportation is allowed, so battery operated cars are used. There is regular ferry service from Hong Kong to discovery. The most enjoyable is chinese, Bay Dragon Boat Carnival. This is during Chinese festival. It becomes even more popular with this race near Victoria Harbor. Hundreds and thousands of riveters enjoy when the top boat athlete battles it out to Hong Kong International Dragon boat race. People enjoy their cold beer and ice cream and cheer for their favorites.{It reminds me of the famous snake boat race in Kerala in Alleppy, Called NEHRU TROPHY in India}.

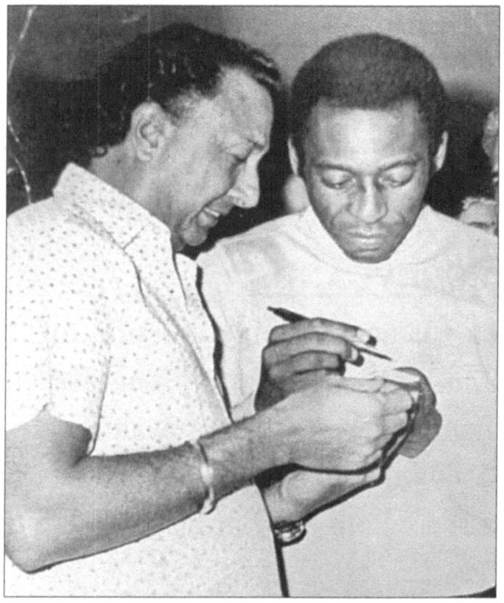

PELE IN 1977 Sept, IN CALCUUTA WITH COSMOS CLUB TEAM.

Well, trip to Hong Kong in four days is not enough but travelers/tourists always look forward to visit again. These are valuable memories, which I wanted to share with my readers. Here, I almost forgot to mention my Historic Flight from HKG to Calcutta insep.1977 with US COSMOS FOOT BALL CLUB, with Great PELE as its Capt. Well, during the flight I did not get much opportunity to Meet Great BLACK PEARL, as PELE was known but

Luckily, we were Staying in the same hotel in GRAND in Calcutta. As the luck would have it, same evening, the Consul General of US Embassy, had thrown a party in the Grand Hotel for Cosmos Club, as the next Evening was the Football Friendly Match With Calcutta `s famous Team MOHUN BAGAN, in EDEN GARDENS Stadium with a capacity of 90000 people. Imagine Calcutta withFoot ball Crazy fans. Only fortunate ones could get TKTS to a have a Glimps of great Pele. One of the Players[Many Cosmos team Players were from Different European countries, who had big names] had become quite friendly With one Yugoslav Player named DIMItri v`iec`, hope my spellings are right during our Flight as I Showed him the cockpit. He met me in the evening in the Hotel Lobby and Invited me to join the party with my crew. I was surprised but requested, if he would Introduce me with Great PELE. He assured me the meeting, so we joined the Party. It was a great party many Govt.

Luminaries too were invited as guests. Well, after some time Pele Entered the Hall with hisBrazilian Blond wife Marriane, Photographers had stormed him for pictures, he was smiling and meeting people. There seemed no chance meeting him. I called my friend Dimitri, who had invited us and asked him, if it was possible to meet PELE. He said,'Wait', here. He went to PELE and steered him towards me and Told him, this was our Capt. Who flew us from HKG.Pele smiled greeted me and got himself photographed with me and my crew. He told that D`mitri, Cosmos team player to bring me for the match, it was 24th sep.1977 with him as his guest. WOW, can any one ever think, in Calcutta, that too a match with Mohan Bhugan as PELE`s Guest. It was a dream come true. Well, we had drinks / dinner in the party and promised to be there in the lobby next evening to travel in the same coach with Pele and his team to the Eden Gardens when we boarded the coach with PELE to go for the match, I saw a teenager, in his attempt top get pele`s autograph, was clinging to the window of the coach, a cop hit this boy with a baton and the boy started bleeding. Pele saw that and ordered the coach to stop. He went out to the boy and signed his auto graph this sent the crowd in a frenzy On this my article was published in MIRROR news paper on June 18th 2006 It had an heading PELE with heart of GOLD.. [Pictures enclosed]I can never forget sittin g next to Pele in the coach. I watched the match with other players from a special Gallery and returned with the

cosmos team back to the hotel. Next afternoon, flew back to Mumbai. I am, sure my readers enthused for foot ball, would be thrilled to read this and enjoy the pictures enclosed. These of Glorius incidents in my life as an airline pilot. Thank full to God that even after 45 yrs, I remember the names, places, incidents. These are very vivid in My memories.

CHAPTER – 15

INDIAN OCEAN ISLAND OF MAURITIUS:

VVIP FLIGHT WITH LATE MRS INDRA GANDHI, PM OF INDIA VISITING MAURITIUS AND MOZAMBIQUE.

I have very sweet memories of this Indian Ocean island with Port Louis as its capital. Its known for its beaches, reefs and lagoons. Rainforests, waterfalls, hiking trails and wild life. The everlasting memory in my mind is my VVIP flight with the- then Indian Prime Minister on board and she was a remarkable lady, Mrs. Indira Gandhi. She was known for mercurial temper and a person of great likes and dislikes and as her pilot on this flight had to be more careful. After this remarkable flight one of my articles in Indian Newspapers was published which was about this journey. " BOUQUETS or Brickbats" which was highly liked by the readers. (copy enclosed) She was on an official visit to Mauritius and Mozambique, Africa. This Prime Minister visit was from the 23rd of August, 1982. The PM of Mauritius was Anuradh Jagan Nath. Her object of this visit was the focus on the Indian ocean. This was her third visit to Mauritius, earlier in 1970 and 1976.

She had proved to be an important ally in Indian Ocean and support for Mauritius today. Its importance is more in view of CHINESE expansion plans.

My fond memories of a flight to Mauritius with Mrs. Indira Gandhi, PM of India, needed all the preparations of security, planning, weather, flight time, etc. to keep the door opening time of the aircraft after landing in Mauritius is of paramount importance as the host country arranges the reception with their PM, in attendance. So everything is meticulously planned including taxi time to the Taximan for the reception.

I have very sweet memories of this Indian Ocean island with Port Louis as its capital. Its known for its beaches, reefs and lagoons. Rainforests, waterfalls, hiking trails and wild life. The everlasting memory in my mind is my VVIP flight with the-then Indian Prime Minister on board and she was a remarkable lady, Mrs. Indira Gandhi. She was known for mercurial temper and a person of great likes and dislikes and as her pilot on this flight had to be more careful. After this remarkable flight one of my articles in Indian Newspapers was published which was about this journey. " BOUQUETS or Brickbats" which was highly liked by the readers. (copy enclosed) She was on an official visit to Mauritius and Mozambique, Africa. This Prime Minister visit was from the 23rd of August, 1982. The PM of Mauritius was Anuradh Jagan Nath. Her object of this visit was the focus on the Indian ocean. This was her third visit to Mauritius, earlier in 1970 and 1976. She had proved to be an important ally in Indian Ocean and support for Mauritius today. Its importance is more in view of CHINESE expansion plans.

My fond memories of a flight to Mauritius with Mrs. Indira Gandhi, PM of India, needed all the preparations of security, planning, weather, flight time, etc. to keep the door opening time of the aircraft after landing in Mauritius is of paramount importance as the host country arranges the reception with their PM, in attendance. So everything is meticulously planned including taxi time to the Taximan for the reception.

Well, we were off from Delhi airport in the night with PM and her entourage our door opening time given was 7:30am. All was fine, good weather and the VVIP resting. Early morning, when I was an hour away from destination I found the wind pattern had changed and I was gaining about 10 minutes. I tried to lose time but it seemed difficult so it was little worrisome. I started sweating as landing earlier would be very embarrassing for the host country for their PM being present at the right time. I thought of paying a visit to the PM in her special cabin. I was delighted to see her sitting next to the window and looking outside. After my respects and 'namaste' she smiled and asked about the flight, weather, etc. Now was the important moment I wanted. I told her about the beauty of Mauritius Island from the Air and if she would like an aerial view, when we reach.

Mauritius Island and I could go around it at 2,000 so that would give her a clear view of the island. My heart was beating fast, what she had to say- "yes, I would love to see." Most joyous for me to lose that extra time so landed on time and door opened at 7:30am. VVIP flight can bring flowers on the brickbats, captain has to take formalities in to account.

LATE PM. MRS. INDIRA GANDHI`S VISIT TO MOZAMBIQUE.

Another unforgettable incident after the flight from Mauritius to Mozambique after a layover in

Mauritius for 2 days. Same thing , the host country had arranged reception at Maputo Airport with their head of state in attendance[SENIOR MARCHEL}. As the Indian PM stepped down the ladder Mr. Marchel stepped forward and hugged her and planted a slight kiss on her cheek.

Wow, that was not expected as per the Indian protocol but since Mozambique was under the PORTUGUESE rule for a long time it was in order. Mrs. Gandhi was seemingly embarrassed and stepped back (this was captured in my camera from the Aircraft. It is enclosed for my readers to see.) After a day, on departure, Mr. Marchel was seen shaking hands with her from two feet probably, Indian protocol must have been briefed to their counterparts. Such incidents, during my tenure as VVIP pilot are most memorable. On return, I again met Mrs. Gandhi during the flight back, she was very pleased to talk to me and agreed to get herself photographed by me (photograph enclosed).

MRS. INDRA GANDHI.{MOST CHERISHED VVIP FLIGHT WITH LATE PRIME MINISTER INDIRA GANDHI}.

I found her to be a very likeable, beautiful person. I had many occasions to fly her to US for the UN meetings later on. On my flight to Africa and Indian ocean island of Mauritius AND MOZAMBIQUE, it's Capitol MAPUTO, WELL HERE AFTER MAURITIUS FLEW HER TO MOPUTO, THIS COUNTRY MOZAMBIQUE ACHIEVED ITS INDEPENDENCE FROM PORTUGUESE IN 1975 after almost a decade of war of Independence against Portuguese from colonial rule then its military rule started with SAMORA MACHEL, WELL AFTER LANDING IN MAPUTO, COL MACHEL WAS THERE TO RECIEVE MRS. GANDHI. I WAS WATCHING FROM THE COCKPIT TO CAPTURE THE RECEPTION WITH MY CAMERA, AS MRS GANDHI STEPPED DOWN, COL MACHEL CAME FORWARD AND PLANTED A KISS ON HER CHEEK, A WAY OF GREETING IN THEIR COUNTRY. OH, MRS GANDHI WAS TAKEN BY SURPRISE AND STEPPED BACK. I HAD CLICKED THAT MOMENT IN MY CAMERA {PICTURE ENCLOSED FOR READERS TO SEE}AFTER WARDS INDIAN PROTOCOL PROBABLY BRIEFED THE MOZAMBIQUE PROTOCOL THAT IT WAS NOT DONE AS PER INDIAN TRADITIONS, SO AFTER A STAY OF ONE DAY, NEXT MORNING ON

DEPARTURE, I NOTICED COL MACHEL SHAKING HAND FROM 2 FEET. WELL, SUCH MEMORIES ARE KEPT IN MY PHOTO ALBUM.[AFTER THE RETURN OF MRS GANDHI TO DELHI, I SENT HER HER PICTURES TAKEN IN THE AIRCRAFT, PICTURE TAKEN DURING THE FLIGHT, I REQUESTED HER FOR MY MEMORY, SHE SMILED AND POSED FOR ME. I SENT HER THE PICTURES THEN RECEIVED HER LETTER OF THANKS}.

LETTER FROM PRIME MINISTER`S OFFICE TO ME.

MY SURPRISE ONE DAY RECD. A LETTER FROM PRIME MINISTER`S OFFICE, MRS GANDHI THANKED ME. ONLY HER PICTURES IN THE AIRCRAFT, NOT THE ONE ON ARRIVAL IN MOPUTU, WHERE SHE WAS KISSED BY LEADER OF MOGADISSIO AS DESCRIBED ABOVE] **SEYECHELES ANOTHER BEAUTIFUL ISLAND, BEAUTIFUL BEACHES AND NICE AQUATIC LIFE IN THE INDIAN OCEAN.**

I had another memorable incident, once after take-off, the boeing 707 aircraft, I was checking another Capt on this sector, lost pressurization after flying for 30 minutes. So I had to take over from the Pilot under check with me and landed back. This entailed a stopover for 2 days as the spares had to be flown from India. This gave me and the crew to enjoy the sights of this beautiful island with Golden Beaches, here warm turquoise water with palm fringed. White sandy beaches and tropical weather, invites hordes of tourists, especially French as the local language is mixed with French and creol language, lot of French color in the local population. This island is known for scuba diving, crystal clear lagoons and full aquatic life. Other beautiful islands in the Indian ocean are Rodrigues and Reunion Islands all with French culture and flair European tourists enjoy its sunshine in Autumn south of Equator.

Mauritius is a real holidays destination. Its idyllic and stunning beaches, waterfalls, rivers, craters, and magnificent landscape. Its culture is mixed with Creole, French, and Indian. People are very friendly and hospitable, main cultivation and export is sugarcane. There are many five-star hotels on the beaches. Main towns are Curepipe and Port Louis- its capital. There are many cruises to venture out and lots of water sports, speed boats, paragliding and other activities. There were direct flights of Air India by weekly from Bombay and I had done many of them.

Then an opportunity came my way when Air Mauritius was started and they needed flight crew from Air India. I was detailed to fly Air Mauritius for 4 months, two months based in Mauritius and 2 months in Nairobi. This flight was from Johanesburg, Mauritius, Nairobi, Rome, London and back.

British crew was flying the first leg and Indian flight crew with French cabin crew took over to London and back. This stay in Mauritius got me many Indian Mauritian friends and with them enjoyed the local culture, food, traditions and many boat cruises in the sea. Beautiful stay in Mauritius, then was posted in Nairobi by Air Mauritius for another 2 months.

Another beautiful island of Maldives awaited in my wish-list but the opportunity never came. Mauritius has many beautiful shopping malls, many in Curepipe and Port Louis but heard in the last 30 years, lot of changes have taken place and tourism has increased many folds. Lots of underwater activities for the tourists. Well, the list to mention more is never-ending.

MY TENURE ON DEPEPUTATION FOR 4 MONTHS IN 1979 TO AIR MAURITIUS.

I was working for Air Mauritius in 1979 on deputation from Air India. I was stationed in Mauritius for 2 months then moved to Nairobi for 2 months. In Nairobi, had the occasion to visit many of the beuaitful places like the Lake Nakura and TSVO National Park. Always wanted to visit MASAI MARA but lack of time and no opportunity could not do so. FULLY DESCRIBED IN CHAPTER ON NAIROBI ABOUT THE BEAUTIFUL PLACES AROUND NAIROBI.

FLYING LATE PRESIDENT DANIAL ARAP MOE OF KENYA.

I was deputed for a flight to NAIROBI to fly Late President of KENYA DANIAL ARAP Moe to India. It was great honour and pictures were taken, my greeting him before

Departure for India at Nairobi Airport.[Picture enclosed for readers to see]. Really, It is such a feeling after retirement, being a VVIP pilot. It is a nostalgia, as the whole scene comes back of such incidents. PICTURE ENCLOSED AT NAIROBI AIRPORT BEFORE DEPARTURE MY GREETING HIM AT THE DOOR STEPS OF THE AIRCRAFT.

FLYING LATE PRIME MINISTER RAJIV GANDHI

I HAD DESCRIBED EARLIER ABOUT FLYING LATE PT. NEHRU, INDIRA GANDHI AND RAJIV GANDHI, ALL THREE PRIME MINISTERS OF THE SAME FAMILY. I WAS DEPUTED TO FLY HIM FROM MOSCOW TO DELHI. HE BEING A PILOT HIMSELF, HAD TO BE MORE CAREFUL DURING MY FLIGHT. I VISITED HIS CABIN DURING THE FLIGHT GREETED HIM WITH RESPECT AND REQUESTED, IF HE WOULD LIKE TO VISIT THE COCKPIT. HE CAME WITH ME AND SAT IN THE CO-PILOT SEAT OF 707 BOING AND ASKED ABOUT THE INSTRUMENTS ETC. THEN LEFT, SO I REQUESTED FOR HIS PICTURE IN THE AIRCRAFT, HE POLITELY AGREED.[PICTURE ENCLOSED] HE WAS A VERY KIND HUMBLE PERSON.

CHAPTER – 16

THERAN

As I may have mentioned earlier, I had the knack of getting stuck in situations in like a military coup, civil unrest as well as a civil revolution.

This time it was in Tehran when AL- Khomini the local head of Shias, who lived in France was Islamic head, was against the Pehlavi Regime and wanted Iran to become Islamic Republic, this made the people to revolt against Shah Pehlvi of Iran, who fled the country and Ataula Khomini was brought to Tehran. I was stuck during this overthrow of Shah dynasty in 1975. Shah had fled on the 16th of January, 1979 when I was in Tehran during my layover of Air India flight. It was all a chaos and no flights as the airport was closed. I cannot forget one incident, the day after Shah Pehlvi Fled the county. We in the Hotel had no Knowledge, Next morning I along with my co-pilot and Engineer went on the main street as usual to Visit a bar, for a glass of beer and famous Iranian food, suddenly huge crowd had gathered with slogans against Royal Dynesty and within no time, Shooting started, I was just wondering, what happened, suddenly saw one person about 10 meters ahead was hit by a bullet and he fell down. I was watching him, when he got up with his right eye hanging in his hands. My co-pilot shook me and said sir, dot stand lets get back to the hotel as firing is going on. Some how through the back lanes, we reached the hotel. It was completely ransacked. The bar, lobby all over glass pieces, broken down every thing. We were shocked and were stuck there, no restaurant, no food. With God`s grace found out the back door of the hotel, opening in to a lane, where one indian Diplomat attached with some UN agency was living there. We visited him and requested for Food as there was no place to go. He was living alone and offered us food for next few days till Air india managed to get us out. This nightmare kept haunting me for many days. There were thousands of Indians stuck, along with other nationalities.

After great difficulty, Air India managed to get us out of Tehran when I was sent to Bahrain for few days to operate Air India flights in Tehran to bring out Indians who were stuck there. I did many flights in most difficult circumstances with no Air Traffic Control over the Iranian Airspace. Many countries were flying to evacuate their people so I had to conduct my own Air Traffic Control with the other Aircrafts in the Iranian airspace. It was a real great effort and was successful. I was later appreciated for my efforts in different situations to evacuate lots of Indian on several Air India flights. I got a letter of

Commendation from my Director of Operations, Air India. (Letter copy has been enclosed) During Mohd Shah Pehelvi`s time Tehran wascompletely different. Most fashionable alike Paris. Good restaurants, night life, Bars even Race course at that altitude. Beautiful Museaum with Peacock Golden Throne and other Valuable Artifacts. I always enjoyed my stay during Air India Layovers. One could enjoy the Dryfruits for shopping.People were very friendly. Women were most beautiful, Fashionable. Well life has changed completely after King Pehlvi`s abdication. Earlier Air India Crew on Layover Period, used to stay in a posh Hotel on Pehlavi Ave, it was the most beautiful long Avenue, full of modern shopping area with good resturants. Most scenic towards the west, one could see the snow clap mountain and a small rivelet flowing through this Main road. Now after the new regime take over, its name is changed to Valiasr, it was the longest street in Tehran. Both sides of the street covered with beautiful trees.

Other famous cities of Iran, are Shiraz, Isfahan Kashan, Tabriz, Yazd and Mashad even forgot about Kerman. Infact Terhran is towards the south.. Iran has natural wealth in its Oil and Natural gas supply. the Iranian Language is Persian or called Farsi. Many world famous poets were of Iranian descent. One can never forget Ferdouwsi, he was known for writing Shah Nama, the great Persian Epic. Another great poet, one can never forget was Sufi mystic writer Rumi. I am sure many of my readers heard about Shahnama, it is an History or may call book of Kings. Another famous name was Omar Khyayam, he was a Persian astromer, writer, poet his Rubaiat are very well admired in our modern age. It is well known that Parsi community in India are the descendents from Zoroastrians, who fled Iran to escape religious prosecution by Muslims. Parsis first landed in Gujrat, where they were sheltered by Hindu King. This is a most honest dependable hard working community today, Zoroastrian is one of the oldest religeons. It is commendable, they have preserved their rituals. Parsis normally marry within own community but that thing is no more prevalent. Now vast majority is married outside their community. They are now dwindling in their population.

One thing is amazing that Parsis have a longer living everage age it is around 85 yrs, much longer than any others. May be its in their gene. In india, we have had many famous Personalities, industrial powers like TATAS. Many renown Medical specialist, They are really assets to India. Mainly they are settled in Gujrat and Maharashtra specially in Mumbai. Their worship place is called Agiary Where they worship Fire. The most famous parsi place in is small coastal town called Udvada. It is considered their holiest place. Fire Temple is called Agiary, place of worship. Comming back to Iran, I had My Air india Flights going to Moscow from Delhi, flight path was over Iran and had the fortune of flying over their many famous cities I hope My readers must have enjoyed my deep memories and excerpts from my old diaries with flying experience which is named Wanderlust. Going around the world and learning so much about each country, its culture, traditions, habits and food. I always thank the almighty for being kind with his divinity on me. Lastly, I must mention a few words about Mohd Shah Pehlavi, He fled to take refuge in many countries, even to Bhamas, Panama, USA but eventually took refuge in Egypt given by PM. Anwar EL- Sadat, where he died of cancer. He was buried in AL-Rifa Mosque in Cairo. Shah Pehlavi`s First wife was Princess Fawzia of Egypt, she was also sister of King Farouk Of Egypt, who was later Deported from Egypt by the Military rulers. Later Shah Pehlavi married Second wife, Farha, who lives in france.

Well, another time I was stuck in Beirut during Arab-Israel war of 7 days.

BEIRUT:-

This flow of memories is a flashback are so vivid that I thank the God who always helped me to face different situations as a pilot. This is what I want readers to understand, what a pilot goes though in his flying career.

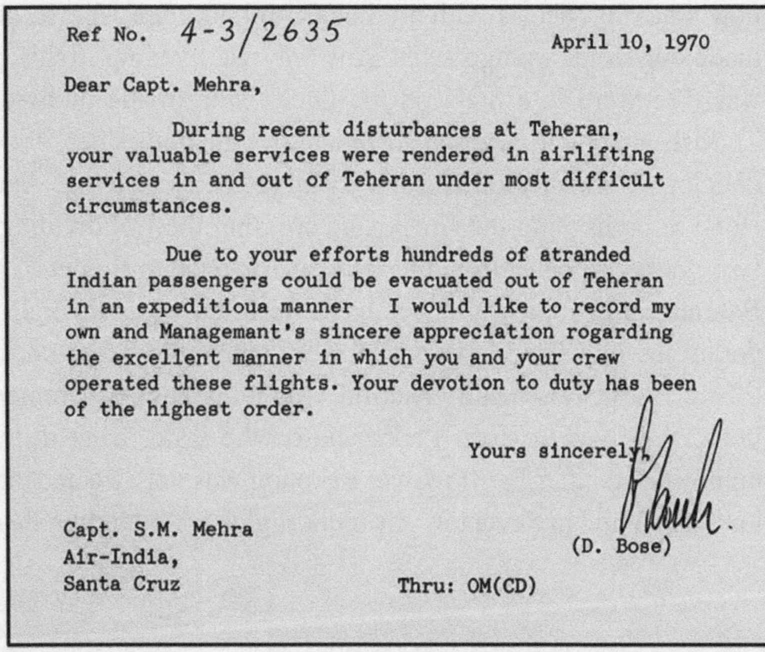

Ref No. 4-3/2635 April 10, 1970

Dear Capt. Mehra,

During recent disturbances at Teheran, your valuable services were rendered in airlifting services in and out of Teheran under most difficult circumstances.

Due to your efforts hundreds of atranded Indian passengers could be evacuated out of Teheran in an expeditioua manner I would like to record my own and Managemant's sincere appreciation rogarding the excellent manner in which you and your crew operated these flights. Your devotion to duty has been of the highest order.

Yours sincerely,

(D. Bose)

Capt. S.M. Mehra
Air-India,
Santa Cruz

Thru: OM(CD)

Beirut, is the capital of Lebanon. It is on the Mediterranean Coast between Israel and Syria dividing the Cedar Mountains. This is where east meets the west. This was fast paced most fashionable. I must admit that the women there were most beautiful and attracted to my mind, they had beautiful complexion and features. I always felt that God almighty took lot of time to use the best material for their production. One could go up the Cedar Mountains in Summer and enjoy the snow then come down to enjoy a swim in the sea with beautiful beaches. Delicious Mediterranean food, with Humous, and kebabs and Khabus. (Picure enclosed) Oh, it reminds me of the most enjoyable days of my layover in IAF days (Flying superconstellation, on military courier duties) and Air India flights were operating from Mumbai-Beirut-London. I would love to mention, During our lay over periods in Beirut. There were beautiful night clubs, were Parisian life and atmosphere. Even casinos and Clubs where special shows, what we see in Paris in Le Pagale, similar shows were there. It was a mini Paris. People so friendly. One could do shopping for house hold items from all over the world there was change alley, where one could change currency in Labenese pounds. Most delicious Labenese food, like Humus, rice pillaf Fattoush Tabbouleh, falafel shawarma most delicious was labenese Kibbeh, enjoyed with drink of Arak. Well it was a laid back mood, with night clubs on the waterfront lebenon was under france till1943. Hence the Parisian feel was there I did get a chance to visit a few, like Dannys and some night shows but all remains a beautiful memory now.

In 1967, while staying in Hilton, near the seashore, I saw a fighter aircraft flying low level over the city. I was surprised as Lebanon had no Airforce. Later, I found myself stuck in a warzone between the 5 Arab nations and Israel on the other side and these were Israeli aircraft making low passes over Beirut. I was worried as my military aircraft full of military spares bringing from Paris and London on these courier flights was parked in the open at the Beirut Airport. One missile from the fighter jet could blow my aircraft to smitherns. Apart from food, this was a serious problem as my flight route was over the mountains in Syria, then Southi Arabia in to Bahrain and then Jamnagar in India. There was war and this airspace was closed. Great difficult situation to get out of Beirut. After 5 days, was allowed to fly at 500ft over the sea to Nicosia in Cyprus. At last got out but now stuck in Nicosia with no money and no help. At last, our military Attache in Beirut made our Hotel arrangements. Any way we lived up to this respite out of all the panic of war. We were in a hotel on the Greek side of the undividing Nicosia into Greek and Turkish sides but we used to move around both sides, food, yujyaras(colorful drinks), delicious Turkish food and not to forget belly-dancing. And then used to return to our Hotel at night on to the Greek side crossing the UN dividing line with our passports . At last, got permissions from the Turkish Airspace to fly out of Nicosia via Turkey, Iran into Bahrain, after refueling at Jamnagar in India. What a flight, never forgot. This life had got all the highs and lows but all were enjoyable. Later on, when things became normal, life in Beirut was again beautiful. Air india flights, I remember, flying while with Air india. We lived in Hotel Phonexcia on the water front in town same Labense food and night life. As after the 1967 war Lebenon was not effected, so again tourism had attracted tourists. While in Seventies Air india flights were landing there.

CHAPTER – 17

EGYPT

I must not forget about the Jewel of Middle east EGYPT. While flying for AIR-INDIA, I had many flights to Cairo and long stay over as the flights were Mumbai cairo-london and return London cairo Mumbai so the crew had enough of existence after life, "the crew with me learnt enough that Life existence after Death pointing to Pyramids and Mummies." All this points towards these pyramids and Mumies pharaohs, had constructed these pyramids as luxury tombs in fact the secrets lies inside the pyramids of giza. There are passageways and chambers inside at the bottom of the pyramids. In the center, is great pyramid of khufu, better to take a guided tour where all explanation is given. As a tourist to Cairo, one can explore many old artifacts, jewellery dresses.

Best is to take a day tour by the river nile, this cruise plus a night dinner cruise in the Nile with best of Egyptian dishes and famous belly dancing well during my stays due to limited timestay, I could not visit Luxur, infact the old prehistoric 500 BC, Egyptian monuments and long history of Egyptian culture could be seen there. Egyptians are very friendly generous people to deal with language is no problem as all speak English.

History of River Nile is another thing to venture in to here in the last if my memory is right, the guide in Giza told me that sphinx is the worlds oldest monument, it is the largest monolith statue on earth well, also it was revealed that Khufu was the second king of 4th dynasty [2543-2436] BC. who was the builder of great pyramid in the centre of the three. Even in Paris I saw luxur obelisk, this 3000 yrs old is located in the centre of place de la concord, it was carved in the reign of Ramesses lay over time to explore the famous

Egyptian places to visit. We used to stay in Hilton on the Nile, beautiful 5 star hotel, from the balcony of the room, one could see all the traffic in the river nile and on the left there was a bridge over Nile connecting new to old cairo. Very close to the hotel was national museam, which had old Egyptian artifacts depicting to Egyptian Prehistoric items .plus mumies and so much dating back to 2500 yrs BC. It is a must visit for tourists then one could go across the bridge over Nile to the old cairo and firstly proceed to GIZA, I would recommend, one should take a day tour with the guide so that one can really know the history of three Pyramids and the great Sphinx these are all prehistoric monuments, decalared as one of the wonders of the world. Well, what I had learnt from the guide that sphinx is a body of lion and head of a human, it was believed as a solar diety or sun God, mythological symbol. It represented courage and strength it was built as a great protector of the pyramids. It was built during the construction of great pyramid of khufu, son of khafre ancient Egyptians profoundly had a belief second, around 1250 BC. Well, lets move on to another beautiful place, hope my readers enjoyed so far one must visitKhan El Khalili, here. Tourists really enjoy their vibrant Bazar, which is like a trove ofEgyptian culture and shopping specially Egyptian items. I always visited Al Hamra where many delicious Egyptian Kababs, were known for. On my return flights During Air india flights, I used to get these packed to bring back home as my children Loved it. There are so many memories about my visits to Cairo, Very peaceful atmosphere and very friendly people. I had heard so much about Luxur but never had time and chance to visit that place, infact the Olden prehistoric History is found there. Very popular tourist place. I loved their Dadasha, a dress for men, most comfortable and brought two for myself home and used to wear at home in the evening, same is available in all Arab countries, infact after many years visited Dubai on a private visit and bought one in white, very comfortable, It is in one piece. Mostly Arabs wear this. Well lets fly to another place with more memories.

CHAPTER – 18

LONDON, MY FAVOURITE CITY

Every tourist feels if he has not visited London he has deprived himself from the core of tourism. London is almost all the Airlines network and hundreds and thousands of tourists arrive and depart from giant ferris wheel for breathtaking view, the London Eye.

I shall start with famous Buckingham Palace, this was built in the 1837 and has been home to the Royal family ever since Queen Victoria. If the Queen is at her residence, one can find out the flagpole atop. On special occasions the Royal Family even emerges o the Central Balcony for the thousands of people waiting outside to catch a glimpse.

CHANGING OF GUARDS EVERY MORNING IN SIDE BUCKINGHAM PALACE GATE

The biggest tourist attraction is changing of guards at 11:30am from April-July the alternate days thereafter. It is a spectacle most colorful with band and march by the Royal Guards for about 40 minutes.

In 1993, the state rooms were opened to the public by tickets and the proceeds were used for the restoration of Windsor Castle. In this tour, one watches the Royal Collections, painting, sculptures, porcelain, period Heathrow and Gatwick Airports, which are packed. I noticed once there was a strike by some of the unions serving Heathrow airport and it put off dozens of airlines with full load of passengers stranded. It was a total chaos so once can imagine how visit to London by every tourist is attractive.

London has so much to offer, its natural museums, London Bridge and Big Ben, Madamme Tussauds, Changing of Guards at Buckingham Palace in the morning and the beautiful sunshine in the Hyde Park to relax, Trafalgar Square, St. James Palace and Tower Bridge and above all Piccadilly Circus which is most vibrant during the day and night. London attracts 15 million visitors each year. Its world famous theatres are always packed. Now after my retirement from Air India, 25 years ago, a new attraction is added, it's a furniture, picture gallery, etc.

Royal mews, once can see royal coaches including a "golden state coach" from 1762 and used for Royal Coronation.

It takes 8 horses to pull it. Then a glass coach for Royal Weddings. One enjoys seeing the Royal Cars, most expensive Rolls Royce limousines, the Phantom, then Bentleys, and Jaguars also on display. This guided tour is very knowledgeable.

I was very lucky to stay as Air India's crew in St. James Court Hotel which was very close to the Buckingham Palace. Just walking distances to visit these sites while walking through famous Victoria Tube Station also just walking distance.

Directly in front of the Palace is large memorial to Queen Victoria, a statue. A tourist can never tire of seeing all these interesting sites with history behind in London, which is the heart of Tourism in Europe. One can see the Parliament House on the bank of river Thames and Waterloo Bridge and Big Ben. A big attraction is the Tower of London. Where every tourist wants to see the Queen Jewels and the world- famous diamond, 'Kohinoor' in the crown placed there.

MAYFAIR THE MOST SOUGHT AFTER BY THE RICH BILLIONAIRS FOR PROPERTIES AS MOST EXPENSIVE. GOOD TO TAKE A WALK AND ENJOY

London is famous for its museums like Victoria and Albert museum, London National History Museum, one can spend a full day there.

Tower of London, it was used for conferment of its many prisoners including the King David-II of Scotland, Princess Elizabeth, Late Queen Elizabeth-I, Sir Walter Raliegh and William Pen. Many famous people were also executed including Henry-VI as well Henry-VIII's wives, well, the guide assures that ghosts are reported to haunt its ramparts and dungeons. Well, better to see the display armor old collection of weapons.

Jewel House, an imperial state crown studded with more than 2800 diamonds and other precious stones, it was made for Queen Victoria in 1837. One can see the famous diamond, "Kohinoor" from India. There are guided tours which are very informative. The transportation for tourists is very good, easy, comfortable and cheap through tubes and buses.

London Eye or its Ferris Wheel. During my private visit to London a few years ago walked to visit the London Eye. It was fascinating to watch whole of London with its marvelous landmarks from there. It is Europe's tallest ferris wheel situated on the south bank of River Thames. Its is 443 feet.

Constructed in 1998 and opened to the public on the 31st of December, 1999. It is better to buy its ticket online for about 23 pounds to avoid long ques at the site and also can book the slot for entry.

Madame Tussauds in London, this is a world-famous wax museum. It has wax figures from Hollywood to Bollywood to Politics to Royal, Performers and stage personalities to Athletes. Once can click all the pictures with these wax figures, looking like actuals. It is situated on the Bakers Street. It has 13 zones and over 300 figures. One can click a selfie with Michael Jackson to the British Royal Family. The best part is the stand between the Royal Family figures for a picture {PICTURE ENCLOSED}. It shows as if you were a part of the royal family and this is most popular with visitors. This is daily opened, in peak tourist season open from 8:30am till 5:00pm in the evening.

Piccadilly Circus, is like Times Square in New York. People from all over the world connect to this place. It is very popular and estimated that over 100 million people walk through Piccadilly Circus in a year. It is most famous intersection connecting Regent Street, Shaftesbury Avenue, Covent Street, Glass House Street, Haymarket and many more. This junction is called Piccadilly Circus. It is also famous for its digital advertising and lights. These are on 24/7 hours but were turned off on the occasion of death of Sir Winston Churchill, Lady Diana and to mark the Earth Hour. In the middle of this place, there is a Shaftesbury memorial fountain to commemorate famous philanthropist Lord Shaftesbury. This is very busy and expensive area.

One can take a stroll through the Regent Street to come to Oxford Street. This area of Piccadilly really comes to life at night, with lights and theatres. One can take a stroll to historic Leicester square along the Covent Street, Piccadilly theatre, Prince of Wales Theatre, Queens Theatre. There are many to enjoy a play and Soho's theatre district, they are all walking distance. All pubs and eating joints are everywhere in Piccadilly. The plays cater to everyone from Musicals, Plays, Family shows, etc. My advice to friends is not to miss these theatres, neither in London or New York. They are worth to remember. Sometimes very famous Hollywood stars are acting in one of the Plays.

NEW YEARS EVE IN LONDON, is again a very big attraction for the tourists in Trafalgar Square, most popular public space to celebrate New Year's Eve. Fireworks but now I am told the best place to watch the fireworks on New Year Eve is from a London Eye. So, the Big Ben chimes at midnight the fireworks start to welcome the New Year. Well, all the pubs and clubs are bustling with crowds to celebrate, many of them being tourists. London Bridge and Tower Bridge are also big attractions from there to watch the fireworks. How much, can I describe London as if I did 3 postings there as Air India Pilot and enjoyed the most. In fact, flying 747 at night from New York, Kennedy Airport to London Heathrow whole night and landing early morning at Heathrow used to get homecoming feelings. I remember, once flying to London I was about 150 miles from the Irish coast I saw something so natural, the Moon was just disappearing on the horizon and in the same frame sun was just rising on the horizon. Both so close to each other to shake their hands. This picture imbibed in my head forever. Those days in the early 1990s I did not have a mobile to to capture . As an Airline International Pilot had the pleasure to watch the nature so close. (New York to London was coming from West to East).

LONDON UNDERGROUND TUBES, known to be the most efficient underground public rapid transit system serving London and adjacent counties. It has 11 lines and daily commuters travelling are estimated to be around 5 million. It is a cheap and most comfortable mode of travel and visitors can commute in all directions of London and visitors can purchase money saving oysters daily travel card or 1-day travel card between zone 1 to zone 6.

Oyster card is for combination travel by Bus, Train and underground in a single day. London Tube network travel maps are available at all Tube Stations, one can easily monitor the stations and different lines on the tubes network plus inter Tube-line stations to change. All information is very simple with different colors given to different lines of underground by the tourists from informative help desks and even in hotels.

It is so pleasurable in Tubes, fully airconditioned with cushion seats with big glass panes to enjoy the outside view. One can even take leisurely walk from Piccadilly Circus via Oxford Street to Bond Street and find famous stores for all the shopping one needs to do.

Transatlantic flights from Europe, Africa or Middle East to North America, Canada, etc are well connected as well.

CHAPTER – 19

USA....CROSSING ATLANTIC FLIGHTS

I had three postings in London, Mainly to operate flights over Atlantic to New York in 707 aircraft and later 747 Jumbo aircraft. Here, to start with, I would like to aquaint my readers with procedures to follow for operation of these flights. Since Hundreds of flights from all over Europe fly to USA and CANADA, so there has to be some controller to follow safety of these flights crossing the atlantic. If there is no proper procedure, there can be a huge unmanageable rush of aircraft and every chance of air collision. Flights from London Heathrow to North atlantic organized Track system Flights from West Europen countries to North America and Canada fly during day time and flights from USA and Canada Fly during Night time. Now the Day flights are controlled by the Controlling station at SHANWICK [IN IRELAND] and return flights from USA/Canada are contolled by Gander[New Foundland]from the other side. All flight tracks are calculated by taking in to Consideration the Jetstreams, the winds at high altitude which blow from west to east. All flights are assigned their tracks Keeping in view the safety as about 1800 flights use atlantic crossing in day and night from all over Europe and USA/Canada.

Most busiest Crossing over Atlantic ocean. Well all airlines send their requirements of flights to Shanwick and Gander and departure times with destinations and accordingly, the controlling stations assign the tracks with Altitude to fly. Each aircraft is assigned their tracks, altitudes over the Atlantic crossing etc. Those days our Air India aircraft were equipped with Inertial Navigation systems and all the reporting positions were fed in to that as per the latitude and longitudes so that could be reported to the controlling authorities SHANWICK AND GANDER, each aircraft was given the tracks separating laterally by about 60 miles same altitudes separation by 2000 feet so flight safety was maintained and each aircraft hadf to maintain their speed to come over the reporting points at time. I am noit going in to technical details as this little information is only for my readers to have some knowledge while flying from east to west over the atlantic ocean and viseversa. Though passangers are not in the knowledge how hundreds of aircraft fly to gather from Europe, Africa etc to north America/Canada and how airsafety is maintained. This is always good to know for passengers, so with peace of mind they enjoy their flights. Well little bit more to know, when these aircraft cross the halfway over atlantic in their flights the controlling authority changes to Gander in new found land on the west coast and that authority diverts the aircraft accordingly to flights going towards CANADA and flights for Kennedy or Other airports in America. It is very interesting and I feel this knowledge by my readers would be welcome. I shall not delve in to other procedures in case of any emergency in flight, how systems work but reassure my readers that all are taken care of in the flight.

NORTHERN LIGHTS, CALLED ARORA BORALIS IN SOUTHERN HEMISPHERE THESE LIGHTS ARE CALLED ARORA AUSTRALIS.

HERE I WOULD LIKE TO MENTION MY EXPERIENCEING TWO FLIGHTS WHICH WERE FLOWN BY ME FROM NEW YORK JFK TO LONDON. ONE WAS FLOWN IN JAN 1989.

I was given the northern routing via HALIFAX Nova Scotia near Scanadian countries closer to Norway etc, in short upper northern latitude. After flying for about an hour, I experienced beautiful rainbow like lights in the dark sky going from North to South. Most beautiful colours like Pink Blue green yellow, violet etc. Which I had heard earlier from others Called NORTHEN LIGHTS. OR ALSO CALLED ARORAE BORALIS and in Southern Hemisphere it is called ARORAE AUSTRALIS. Really a beautiful Natural Phenomena. I could not believe my eyes to experience such a beautiful sight in the dark sky over the ATLANTIC. I immediately announced on the public system to passengers to watch from the aircraft windows. Some of them requested permission to watch from the cockpit. Well, It happens during winter months in the NORTHEN Hemisphere, later on some one explained to me that when sunspots or solar flares send electrically charged particles in to the space we get a magnetic envelop around our planet earth and they are funneled to the areas around the poles and these particles

when collide with atoms the start emitting colorful lights. Well it was too technically to understand so i only mention them as NORTHERN LIGHTS.

Second Natural Phenomena Experienced again on a New York London flight. I was nearing the Destination when the Darkness slowly turning in to day time early morning, almost 300 miles from the English coast, I saw on the Horizon Moon Setting in and Sun started coming up, almost in the same frame from the air. I could see both of them at the same time. Well, what all The Flying Crews Experience from the cockpit is always memorable in the air. Infact after retirement, I had started writing articles for the news papers and one of this was on NORTHEN Lights Published In HIDUSTAN TIMES dated4 AUG 1996. I was very fond of writing such articles to different news papers on different topics for many years but then stopped. IN 2917, I was coaxed by my family to compile all my experiences during flying days in to a book, let others enjoy and share it. So I started again, Hence this WANDER LUST AROUND THE WORLD STARTED TAKING SHAPE FROM MY PAST MEMORIES AND DIARIES KEPT WITH MANY INFORMATIONS GATHERED VISITING SUCH BEAUTIFUL PLACES ALL OVER SPECIALLY IN EGYPT WHERE WHAT THE GUIDE WAS EXPLAINNING, I WROTE DOWN ABOUT THE HISTORY ON GIZA, ETC. AFTER THE VISIT, I ASKED THE GUIDE TO SIT WITH ME AND EXPLAIN AGAIN SO THAT I COULD RECORD IN MY DIARY. IT WAS WORTH THE EXTRA MONEY HE CHARGED. HERE I WOULD FAIL TO MENTION, ON A VISIT AFTER RETIREMENT TO VISIT MY DAUGHTER IN HOUSTON, IN 1997, During the re election of PRESIDENT CLINTON, I had written many articles abut his first term as PRESIDENT and these were published in HOUSTON CHRONICAL, I HAD MENTIONED THAT IF HE WAS RE ELECTED US WOULD ACHIEVE MORE AND IT WOULD STRENGTHEN INDO US RELATIONS. WISHING HIM BEST IN THE RE ELECTIONS TO BE IN THE WHITE HOUSE AGAIN. Well, all these published cuttings were sent to President Clinton. WOW, HE WAS RE ELECTED AND ON JAN 241997, **LETTER FROM THE PRESIDENT OF USA FROM THE WHITE HOUSE IN MY NAME.**

Surprisingly, I received a letter by PRESIDENT CLINTON FROM THE WHITE HOUSE SIGNED BY HIMSELF, THANKING ME. IT WAS THE GREATEST PRICELESS POSSESSION IN MY HOUSE TILL TO DAY {PHOTOES ATTACHED FOR MY READERS TO SEE THEMSELVES}How many people in our country have received such letters personnel by HEAD OF STATE OF ANOTHER COUNTRY. EVEN THE AMERICAN FRIENDS THEY SEE AND CONGRATULATE ME. I COULD NOT BELIEVE MYSELF THIS WHITE ENVELOPE ON LEFT CORNER WRITTEN ‘WHITE HOUSE”I always bow my head to that DIVINE POWER.

NEW YORK

It is most interesting to know that why America is called land of immigrants. The first immigrants as per the history were Spanish, who landed at st. Augustine Florida in 1565 they also moved to Texas and new Mexico. New York`s Eillis Island, the immigrants landed there in 1892 from Europe and That is why on the east coast Newyork became the GOLDEN GATE. One finds even to day all people from different countries settled there that is why New york has multicultural people, restaurants, foods and what not. There is so much Nto see as a tourist. It was interesting to learn that FIRST PRESIDENT OF USA, GEORGE WASHINGTON, was inaugurated as president in New York. It is interesting to know thatNEW YORK is consisting of Five Boroughs. MANHATTEN, QUEENS, BROOKLYN, STATEN ISLAND and BRONX.Queens is the largest where one finds Newyork JFK airport which is about 16 miles from Manhatten, then LA GUARDIA AIRPORT, which is about 8 miles from Manhatten.Queens is also famous for US OPEN Tennis championship Then its Flushing Meadows also connects to Newyork`s LONG ISLAND interesting to know famous Hollywood actors EddY MURPHY and ANNE HATHWAY were from Queens BROOKLYN BOROIUGH is in the west, quite expensive living there with good restaurants, night life etc. BRONX, is considered to be poor people but famous for YANKEE STADIUM, where base ball champioinships take place, it is famous for JAZZ music, musicians, clubs but Night life is little Rowdy. Famous Hollywood Actress JENNIFER LOPEZ comes from there. BOROUGH of STATEN ISLAND, it is full of parks and Ferry to statue of LIBERTY from there. Famous Hollywood Star, PAUL NEWMAN and GEORGE HARRISON come from here. Well, all such information makes interesting to readers of WANDERLUST. Well, coming back to MANHATTEN, it is the heart of New YORK, with its skyscappers and many iconic Buildings. Let me explain about its MADISON GARDEN, it is famous for many things, sports, concerts, political rallies but mainly for Basketball, it is an areana with capacity of 20,000 people.

It is situated between 7th and 8th AVE. And beyween 31st and 33rd street. Famous NBA basket ball matches take place visitors get access to the players locker rooms also. Here, I must mention that in MADISON SQUARE World heavy weight championships are also held. Like world heavy weight champion SONY LISTON at the age of only 22 became champion in 1964 then famous World heavy weight champion

MOHD. ALI [Originally his name was CASSIUS CLAY but changed it after converting to Islam inhis twenties. He had even won the Gold Medal in light heavy weight catg. In Olympics in ROME in 1960. He had won world heavy weight championship on three occasions. In 1974, famous world heavy weight champion ship called SUPER fight against against Joe Frazier and lost the title Mohd ali was all time great in Boxing, he died in 2016 of Parkinson deases. I remember, he had visited India in 1980 and had exhibition fight with indian boxing champion KEHER singh in Delhi, Mumbai and Chennai. I mentioned about Madison Garden Areana with such historical events. In New York Manhatten another famous place to visit is " TOP OF THE ROCK'it is an observatory on top of ROCKFELER centre for the city views from its 69th and 70th FLRs. Well for most visitors flock to Manhatten 5th Ave. Where all famous stores spread across from 49th to 60th streets. One can find all luxury brands like GucciTIFFANY JEWELLERY STORE, Apple sores, Fashion design, sports wear etc then famous CARTIER, ARMANI, LOUIS VITTON, all on 5th AVE well, visiotors on low budget is always good to visit 5th AVE and take a walk and get the pleasure to see these famous stores I cannot forget the famous Hollywood movie B`fast at TIFFANY, starring AUDRY HEPBURN in 1961. On my visit to Tiffany, I could remember this movie, highly popular I must mention about the FAMOUS BROADWAY, where all famous theatres are located and sometimes Hollywood stars also play there though Tkts need to be purchased in advance. In the evenings is quite crowded and full of theatre goers.

STATUE OF LIBERTY

It is very interesting to know about this world famous Icon. I visited it many times and learnt its history. It is on ELLIS island, Tourist can buy a return TicketFrom Newyork Bay In STATEN ISLAND, by a ferry boat. I was surprised to know the reality of this statue. Infact this was built in FRANCE and gifted to America in 1886 it is about 93 mtrs tall. This signifies the Freedom and opportunity for those immigrants, arriving by sea seeking new world . this statue represents a Roman Goddess and signifies Freedom. The statue has on the crown seven spikes for seven oceans, seven continents of the world. Nearby, one see Ellis Island where early immigrants had landed. Freedom from slavery, colour, creed. Equal opportunities for all. This was made by sculptors in france and diassembled then brought by ship and installed at this place on a Pedestal, Built by American Architects. On visiting this place tourist can read all other information there. This is very famous and tourist always Visit Statue of Liberty. {LEARNT THE HISTORY OF STATUE OF LIBERTY THAT IT WAS MADE IN FRANCE AND SHIPPED TO AMERICA AND REALLY IT IS WORTH KNOWING FOR MY READERS}.

NIAGRA FALLS FAMOUS BETWEEN AMERICA AND CANADA.

It is from Niagra river and it is international border between two countries. On American side the fall is called the Bridal veil and Canadian side in Ontario, it is called horse shoe falls. Almost major part of this fall is beautifully vied from Canadian side. Specially during summer, when colorful lights fall on it. It is really mesmerizing. I visited both the sides for the view.

"My Daughter enjoying at Niagra Falls"

On my air india flights To torronto, it was easy to visit Niagra falls and enjoy the view and during my flights to Newyork, I had the chance to visit and see the beauty of this fall. It is at the foot of city of Buffalo near New york. I was very fortunate to get complimentary two Tkt. from Continental airlines, thanks to our good connections of Air india commercial dept and continental airlines. I went with my wife, on a short holiday of 15 days to new york from India and went to buffalo, stayed in one of the hotels for the night and visited Niagra falls. There are ferry boats for the passengers to take the visitors in this Niagra river and quite close to the falls to experience the thrill in all water droplets falling all over, ofcourse rain coats are provided but the thrill is of boat swinging and going through the foam id indescribable. Since Continental airlines was very kind for the complimentary air tkts on my request From Newyork to buffalo and Buffalo to Orlando, in Florida. And From there to Houston and Newyork, so I could visit all these places in one go within Fifteen days of holidays from Air india. I shall come to explain visiting Orlando and Disney world later. As I had mentioned in this Book, earlier on the chapter on Africa, where during my Air India flight to Zimbabve, I managed to Visit VICTORIA FALLS also but comparitivly, Between the two Niagra Falls is more Visited and enjoyed by visitors.[Pictures of both attached of my visits.

CHAPTER – 20

ON DISNEY WORLD IN ORLANDO

As I had mentioned about Disney World, Every visitor to America on the east coast, would like to visit this famous Place. After enjoying the Buffalo trip to Niagra Falls, we flew By same complimentary Tkts. by Continental Airlines to Orlando to visit Disney World. After landing in Orlando though the Disney world is about 20 miles only but one needs to stay for

atleast few days to enjoy all the theme parks. Infact when we visited almost 30 yrs ago, I found at the Orlando apt. itself through Inquieres counters, one could find different lodges and other cheaper hotels little away, about ten /15 miles away but these hotels provided transportation to Disney world to and fro in the evening back to the hotels, their timmings were fixced so after b`fast in ther morning, all visitors boarded the bus for Disney world and given the return time for pick up. It was very convineient. In Disney world one could buy the daily Tkts or 5 days Tkts with no expiry date. So if not possible to stay for five days one could use rest of the days on next visit or give it to friends for their use. In Disney world, what and how to describe, it's a new world.

"Photos of My Daughters"

With six theme parks, different rides, castles and Micky mouse house and under water theme park. Many resturants and eating places. there are mini trains to carry you visitors to different theme parks. I shall mention about Magic Kingdom, where you enjoy Cinderella`s castle then space mountain but most scaring was Carribian haunted house. My wife felt lt very scarry and wanted to get out. Seven dwarfs and mini train the most enjoyable was Hollywood studios. And more in the same theme park one could enjoyroller coaster ride next day we enjoyed animal kingdom, where including Skeletons l;ike diansores Banshees, lions etc. Then we visited Universal theme park. I had forgotten to mention famous[Epcot center] it is famous for human achievements, like space ship to go around earth, it is like a geodesic round sphere there are many rides but the most liked was Hollywood studios, there are many pavilions depicting different countries. It takes full day atleast to enjoy there, That's why I said Disney world tour is not sufficient for one day or even one week. My wife was thrilled to get herself photographed with Micky Mouse.

DISNEY SEA WORLD:- IT is different Theme Park, With zoo and Aquarium, it is world class enjoyment, real marine life, water theme rides, most enjoyable live shows of sea animals, watching stingray lagoon, Manta acquarium is most enjoyablewild sharks so close behind the acuarium glass. and most enjoyable, it is made in 360 degrees, one can watch below above and sides as if you are under water with them there one must visit theme park exciting rides roller coaster etc. Most important is animal theme park here the aquatic wold is shown alive one important thing would like to mention that sea world is not part of Disney world and it has a separate gated entry and one needs to buy tkts though much cheaper than Disney world during my visit i had found that sr citizens had concession hope it is still there.. infact there most exciting rides we found were in Manta it is so exhilarating that even young ones heard screaming with joy. The Manta ride on the roller coaster is like combination of spinning gliding diving, its an experience when diving with head first face down like nose dive, wow my wife was screaming and swore never to undertake such rides again though i was laughing all the way but inside scared too. As i had mentioned earlier in manta aquarium which completely like a glass dome 360 degrees. All sharks and other mysteries of eye sea world are revealed in that glass dome so close like a finger touch around the visitors as if they come close with their mouths open it is really thrilling. Another stingray lagoon and visiting Atlantis water rides sliding down with water in to a water pond. All thrilling I shall advise my readers if one gets a chance to visit Florida Disney world, do not miss the Sea world one can capture all that in your cameras make videos and keep for memory sake. Well I Think I should move on to another chapter and leave the Disney world and sea world for visitors to explore more when they happen to visit there. New chapter. flying to Houston now to Johnson space Center.. HOUSTON. NASA ALSO KNOWN JOHNSON SPACE CENTER.

CHAPTER – 21

HOUSTON IN TEXAS

I visited HOUSTON many times during holidays as my daughter after her marriage had settled down there, so spent many holidays there. I was very fond of contributing articles on many things to newspapers even in Mumbai. I Houston i used to write articles on various subjects as lot of India population is settled there. DURING RE-ELECTION OF BILL CLINTON AS US PRESIDENT, I had written articles in his favour, published in Houston chronicle and sent those copies to him. After he was elected. He wrote a beautiful letter to me at my daughter`s address on 25 jan,1997. [Picture enclosed] It is prized letter framed on the wall of my living room in Mumbai.

First visit to NASA was in 1982, when i had flown, President of INDIA LATE GYANI ZAIL SINGH FOR HIS HEART BY PASS AND DETAILED TO GO THERE AGAIN after one month to bring him back that time my self and crew were taken due courtesy local AIR INDIA mgr to NASA, Johnson space center it was a very memorable visit as I had the chance to see the Moon Rocks, they were kept in glass case. The US apollo space programme brought back many moon rocks to earth by Neil Armstrong and Alan Shepard in 1969and1971 by Alan Shepard in Apollo 14 mission in 1971 again by Harrison Schmitt during Apollo 17 mission in 1972. Really it quite revealing to me as a pilot that how human beings many things to the space scientists about the moon. Well now years have passed and many countries have reached the moon china and recently Our BHARAT. These space programmes launched by Indian ISRO and other agencies will reveal many more space secrets in future.

I remember when US APPOLO 11 programme was launched and first Moon landing with Neil Armstrong was broadcasted in July 1969, I was in INDIAN AIRFORCE posted at Agra and heard about the landing on Radio and the words uttered by NEIL ARMSTRONG on stepping out on moon, he said"ONE SMALL STEP FOR MAN AND A GIANT LEAP FOR MANKIND." Never thought in my dreams that after joining Air-India, one day i will get a chance as a VVIP pilot flying our President of India to HOUSTON, will get a chance to visit NASA and see myself those white chalky Moon rocks in the glass show case. It was very fortunate most memorable visit.

MY SECOND VISIT TO NASA

This happened on visiting my daughter in HOUSTON in 2015 this was after my retirement from Air-India and one of my private visits since after marriage my daughter had settled in Houston, so our SON IN LAW thought of taking us to NASA Johnson space centre. It had expanded and after the space shuttle which was mounted on 747 aircraft was on display in the open for visitors to enjoy and take pictures[pictures attached in this book for my readers to see for themselves] and it was really like an educational tour, visiting the other things in the space centre including a mockup of the cockpit of space capsul, had chance to enter the cockpit and visualise the feelings.

Well, Houston is a very large city and its importance as many headquarters of US trade centres. Even US oil import/export Hqrs, many sky scrappers and lovely architectures. In US TEXAS, it is very important city. I would like to mention about its Houston medical centre, Houston is a very large city infact 4th largest city in US and considered energy Hub. We had visited Galveston It's an island on the Gulf coast beautiful beach hotels eating joints near the beach it is only about one hour plus drive from Houston. There are other beautiful cities around Houston called greater Houston including San Antonio Dallas Austin etc. only San Antonio is about 3 hrs drive but we really enjoyed full day there not to miss its sea world with many things including roller coasters canal rides never miss the River walk very attractive and most informative.

There are guided boat tours its very relaxing cruise with fascinating sites with city s history. Realy enjoyed the sea world with a fascinating, rides and amusement park. One can see the dolphins, penguins it is one of the largest theme park. There were so much to enjoy specially Spanish culture well one day was quite tiring and we reached back Houston around 10 pm.

TRIP TO DALLAS

Well, it remember in late seventies. there used be most popular English TV serial known as DALLAS. In Mumbai, in the evening, we used to be stuck on to this show and its characters and the daily twist in the story. Now since we got a chance to see Dallas, I requested my son in law to show me that house. this show was aired from 1978 to 1991 it was very popular Prime time soap opera about a wealthy family who owned an oil co.

and a huge cattle ranch. It was shot on a ranch with big mansion. So we visited that was so delighted to see with my own eyes I still remember the Scheming main character in that show called JR. so many other things in Dallas like Fortworth. It has its Tex-Mexican cuisine the distance from Houston to Dallas by road is 240 miles but only about 3 hrs plus. Distance from Houston by car to Austin 165 miles takes about 3 hrs. But must visit Austin.

TRIP TO AUSTIN

It is Texas state Capitol it is also famous fo Live Music of the World it is famous for its university. In fact there are many job opportunities and employment and low cost of living in fact flag of Texas, known as Lone star. I was told that many noble Laureates came from here there THER IS EX PRESIDENT, JBL`s presidential library and Lady Bird, park etc but i did not find more attractions as a tourist so we returned to Houston by night.

SAN ANTONIO

Here, most enjoyable is its RIVER WALK with so much of infor mation and iconic Alamo and TEX-Mexican food. Thrilling theme parks. I think readers should know that a visit to San Antonio, must be top priority visiting Texas its most enjoyable, was river cruises and its sea world theme park.

Thrilling rides exciting adventures encounter with some of the most amazing sea creatures. Amazing roller coasters and splashing rides i was very immersed with sea world marine life home to variety of marine life including orca whales dolphins sea lions beluga whales sea turtles and penguins its sea world is one enjoys sea marine animals rides theme parks next to sea world is Aquatica like water slides drop slides under water grotto i found the best water park in Texas. There was so much fun specially families with children, most enjoyable. I shall advise readers not to miss any opportunity for a visit to San ANTONIO. It has bit of Spanish culture. Its popular basket ball team the SOURS is from here. ITA RODEO rides and FIESTA SAN ANTONIO are an attractions for the tourists. It is only 150 miles from Mexican border. So lot of Mexican Food Culture one can enjoy.

IN 2015, during our visit to Houston, my daughter and family wanted to give us a surprise and planned to take us to New ORLEANS in Lousiana well it is a beautiful place on the Mississippi River near the Gulf of Mexico famous for its festivals MARDI GRAS. In fact known as round the clock night life. It's history is of African French and American mix. Vibrant live music only we missed the famous Mardi Gras as this festival takes place late winter carnival. With costumed parades and street parties. I liked the

French neighbourhood which also known as French Quarter. This is the city`s heart. This is called crown jewel of New Orleans we took a walk in its Bourbon st. Good restaurants. TheMost rememberable trip was to was to famous ALLIGATOR FARM, where so much was new for me that how Alligators are fed and preserved and special boat trips in the lake, visitors in the lake where alligators from 8 feet to small ones come very close to the boat and visitors are given the food for feeding by the boat crew to experience how the alligators jump from water for the feed up to take the food dangling from the hands of the visitors[picture enclosed] it is very scary but an experience of life time i was told that this farm known as Gator Farm also had a crocodile which was 18 feet in this Gator swamp. Where almost 2000 alligators are kept under controlled environment. Guided tour helps in all the information. After spending an hour on the boat trip we returned on the shore and visited the museum nearby where most of the demonstration about alligators is explained, out side ''this museum there is[replica of an alligator in a statue with its mouth opened and visitors are delighted to be photographed by putting there hand in side the open jaw of the alligator[picture attached with my wife, putting hand in the alligator jaw very scarry] then drove back to New Orlean as a dinner cruise was also booked for us by my son in law in the Mississippi river at night.

DINNER CRUISE IN THE MISSISIPY RIVER

Most pleasureable dinner cruise with beautiful bar and dinning tables and one could go up through small steps on to the open deck. The cruise takes about 2hrs the cruise boat moving slowly while visitors can enjoy their drinks and watch other cruise boats passing by music and other entertainment is very enjoyable for the visitors same thing reminded of dinner cruise trips in BKK. Well much more to mention for the readers to enjoy reading and visualising every thing. delicious buffet dinner with genuine Cajun and creole dishes reflecting back ground of the residents enjoying the cruise ship moving slowly on can carry his drink on the open deck and sip and enjoy the cruise there are many cruise ship tour agencies one can choose well all was arranged by my son in law as he himself was very informative.

I must admit that there being so much on the east coast of USA that i never missed going over to the west coast though if opportunity came i would have definitely visited at least LAS VEGAS its casinos and night clubs but could not avail this opportunity and during my flying days with Air India the flights to USA were only few To JFK, new jersy and Chicago and to Canada only to Toronto later on many flights were added to San Francisco Washington etc Well i did enjoy my flights to these places with good long layovers so could avail the opportunity for sight seeing. One flight i still remember during severe winter to Toronto.

CHAPTER – 22

TORRONTO IN CANADA. TORRONTO FLIGHTS.

Landing on snowy day though the Runway was cleared but Taxi tracks were snowy one had to be very careful and use mininimum brakes as the aircraft starts skidding and while taking off though aircraft were cleaned from snow but near the take off point aircraft were to stop under an arch, where steam spray from both sides was sprayed to clear any bit of snow and were given five mts to take off so it was safe for the flight. What an experience during my 40 yrs of Flying carrier. My one pleasure during my layover periods in Toronto was visiting NIAGRA FALLS FROM THE CANADIAN SIDE, I had some Indian Friends living in Toronto so during one of my layover period, i requested them for watching NIAGRA FALLS in the evening, since it was only about 80 miles, they took me in their car and wow what a beautiful sight as the sun sets all those colorful lights come on the water falling, it was really long lasting sight. The crowd there waiting for this and clapping and taking pictures. We spent more than 2 hrs and then returned to the hotel in Toronto. Only regret was that my wander lust was not possible to cover CHINA and south AMERICA. Well 85% coverage was good enough for my readers to relax with this book and visualize each place with the writer and feel the experience as they were with me travelling around. TORRONTO.

Well, I had done many flights in AIR INDIA and had made many Indian friends there, sply in cities of Brampton and Scarborough, mainly from Punjab and Haryana settled there long long ago. They took me to Gerard India Bazar once and showed like mini India shops restaurants Indian typical punjabi food. I met many people settled there from even Pakistan and Even Nepal, I was so surprised. I could not visit Vancouver as no AI flats and very far away but many Indians settled there.

CN TOWER IN TORRONTO.

This is much visited TOWER IN TORRONTO. It is 33 stories and 447 meters in height. My friends told me that on a clear day, when visibility is good one could see NIAGRA FALLS, which is about 100 miles away, On my visit to this tower weather was good but I could only see the white water Foams in the air, may be this is water the locals still claim that Niagra falls are visible, but any way enjoyed the food in one the restaurants, enjoyed the garden around. Many things there which i visited have very dim memory now. My hotel was not very far from there so I could visit many other places with my Indian friends another thing which i saw first time was their SKY DOME with a retractable roof, it is over a big stadium where base ball games and championships are held there base ball team blue jays are quite famous well, my friends took me there to show it from inside, it has a capacity of more than 30000 people but main thing what i liked was its all weather retractable dome, a new thing for me in the nineties.

Many concerts etc do take place well after retirement, what ever was in my beautiful memory and information collected in my diaries, i thought of putting in a book for readers to enjoy and relax hope people like it.[What ever pictures, I could trace with me about these places are enclosed for readers to see for themselves. THANKING ALL MY READERS PUBLISHERS AND PEOPLE WHO HELPED ME IN THIS HARD WORK OF SEVEN YEARS TO BRING SOME SATISFACTION IN MY OLD AGE. SPECIALLY MY FAMILY DAUGHTERS, GRAND DAUGHTERS, WHO COAXED ME TO FINISH THE BOOK AND FRIENDS LIKE PRATEEK, WHO HELPED ME IN THE LAST STAGE TO SUMMERISE IT.

Thanking all my readers publishers and people who helped me in this hard work of seven years to bring some satisfaction in my old age. Specially my family daughters, grand daughters,who coaxed me to finish the book and friends like prateek, who helped me in the last stage to summerise it.

Thanks to my dearest nephew rajnish chopra in lucknow, who coaxed me to finish my memoirs and helped in the formation of this book.

Thanks to dear Prateek Tripathi, who like a son with all the knowledge to summerise in to chapter wise shaping it in to the present book for my readers to enjoy.